Classics Alive!

Late-Intermediate Works
by 14 Important Composers of Standard Teaching Literature

Compiled and Edited by
Jane Magrath

Classics Alive! Book 3 offers teachers and students a wide selection of literature to help pace musical and technical development evenly and with ease. The book presents appropriate teaching literature by 14 composers who wrote inspirationally for the intermediate student. The pieces in this book are primarily from Levels 7 and 8, according to Jane Magrath's *The Pianist's Guide to Standard Teaching and Performance Literature* (from which the leveling chart on this page is taken).

The pieces in this book were primarily selected because the music is of high quality, rewarding and enjoyable to play. This collection represents some of the most inspired compositions created at these levels, and keeps these "classics alive" for us today! Studying these works will give students a solid foundation in the best literature available at their level, and will prepare them to proceed to more advanced music. The pieces are easy to learn, rewarding to play and sound great! Enjoy!

Jane Magrath

Editorial note

Fingering throughout the book is editorial. Dynamics and articulation are editorial for most of the pieces from the Baroque and Classical periods. Editorial markings and pedaling were added sparingly and in a spirit of helping the performer realize the score efficiently and stylistically. All suggestions strive to steer the performer in the direction of the most stylistically appropriate performance possible.

Leveling of Literature—Reference Chart for Grading
Levels 1–10, Beginning to Early-Advanced Levels

Level 1	Bartók *Mikrokosmos,* Vol. 1
Level 2	Türk *Pieces for Beginners*
Level 3	Latour Sonatinas; Kabalevsky *Pieces for Young People,* Op. 39
Level 4	*Anna Magdalena Bach Notebook;* Gurlitt *Album for the Young,* Op. 140; Tchaikovsky *Album for the Young,* Op. 39
Level 5	*Anna Magdalena Bach Notebook;* Sonatinas by Attwood, Lynes; Menotti *Poemetti*
Level 6	Clementi *Sonatinas,* Op. 36; Burgmüller *25 Progressive Pieces,* Op. 100
Level 7	Kuhlau and Diabelli Sonatinas; Bach easier *Two-Part Inventions;* Bach *Little Preludes;* Dello Joio *Lyric Pieces for the Young*
Level 8	Moderately difficult Bach *Two-Part Inventions;* Beethoven easier variations sets; Field Nocturnes; Schumann *Album Leaves,* Op. 124; Schubert Waltzes; Turina *Miniatures*
Level 9	Easier Bach *Three-Part Inventions;* easiest Haydn Sonata movements; easiest Mendelssohn *Songs Without Words;* easiest Chopin Mazurkas
Level 10	Bach *Three-Part Inventions;* easiest Chopin Nocturnes; Beethoven *Sonatas,* Op. 49, 79; Mozart *Sonata,* K. 283; Muczynski *Preludes*

Appreciation is extended to Morty and Iris Manus, E. L. Lancaster, and Carol Matz for their support.

ISBN-10: 0-7390-4499-0
ISBN-13: 978-0-7390-4499-5

Table of Contents

Suggested Order of Study

Easier selections

More difficult selections

Prelude in D Minor

BWV 926

Johann Sebastian Bach

17
cresc.
21
mf
dim.
25
p
29

33
cresc.
37
f
41
rit.
f ad libitum
45
a tempo
p

Prelude in D Minor

BWV 940

Johann Sebastian Bach

Sonata in F Major

K. 78

Domenico Scarlatti

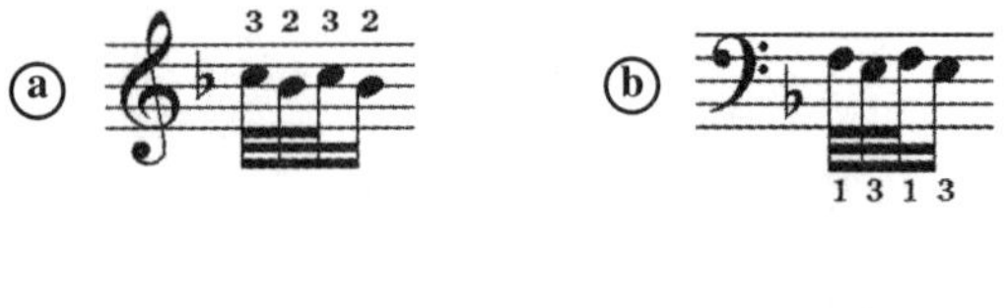

29
mf
34
cresc.
f
39
tr
45
Minuet
p
53

Sonata in G Major

K. 391

Domenico Scarlatti

30
36
42
49
55

Sonata in C Major

K. 309

Domenico Scarlatti

27
mf
cresc.
32
mp
37
f
42
mf
mp
47
mf
p
f
c
d

52
f
57
mp
62
68
73
mf

78
dim.
f
83
mp
88
cresc.
93
mf
mp
98
f

Sonata in A Minor

K. 149

Domenico Scarlatti

ⓐ 

ⓑ A short appoggiatura: 

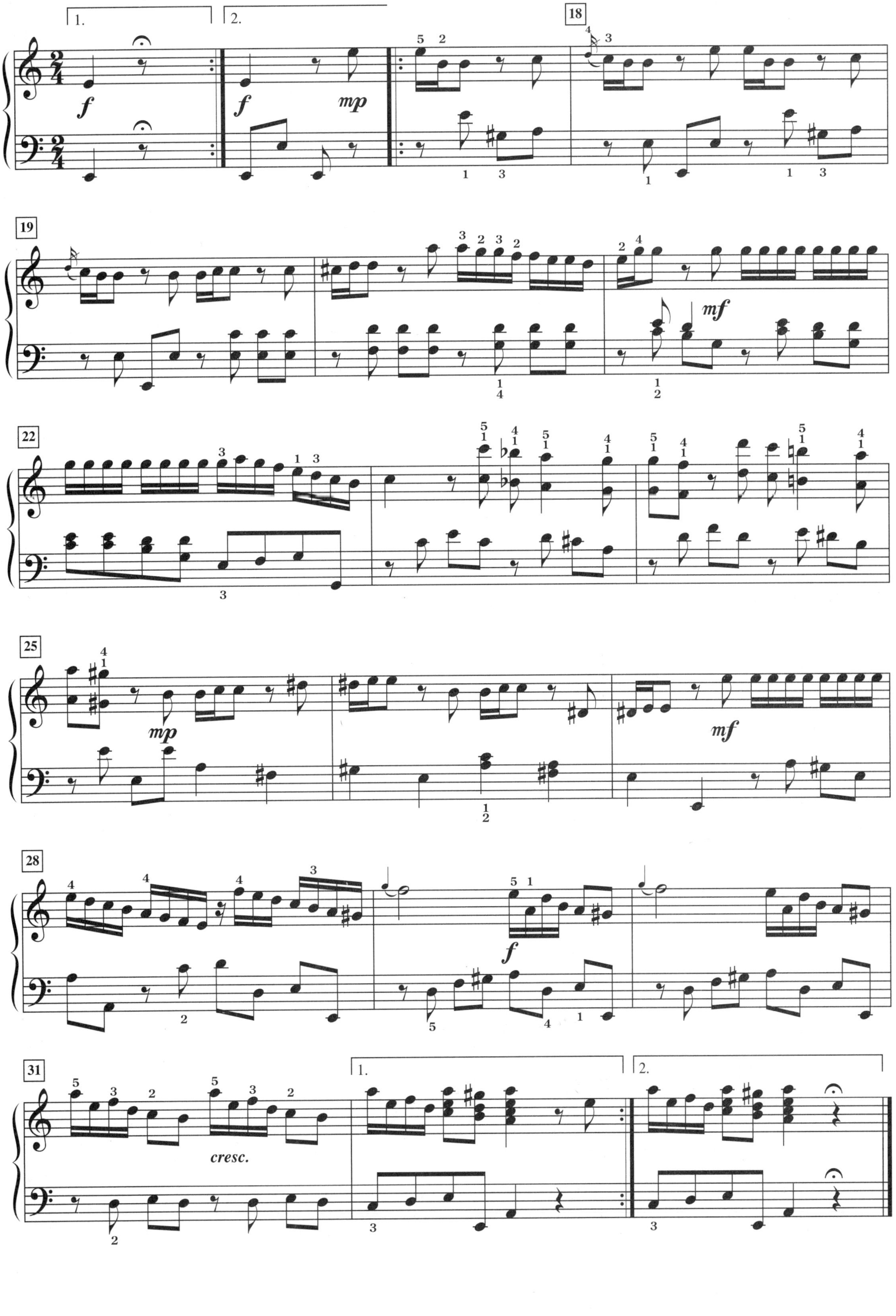
1.
2.
18
19
22
25
28
31
cresc.

Viennese Sonatina No. 1 in C Major

(first movement)

(transcribed from Five Divertimenti, K. 439b)

Wolfgang Amadeus Mozart

The *Six Viennese Sonatinas* were not originally composed by Mozart for the piano. They are transcriptions for piano, by a contemporary of Mozart, of the *Wind Divertimentos* K. 439b composed by Mozart in 1783. It is unknown who arranged the divertimentos for piano. These piano versions have become quite popular today in the piano version and stand on their own in terms of musical quality in the arrangements. Due to the quality of the music and their acceptance in the Classical piano teaching repertoire, they are included in this collection. (These are the only transcriptions included in any piano editions by Dr. Magrath.) *Classics Alive*, Book 3 contains four delightful movements from the *Viennese Sonatinas*.

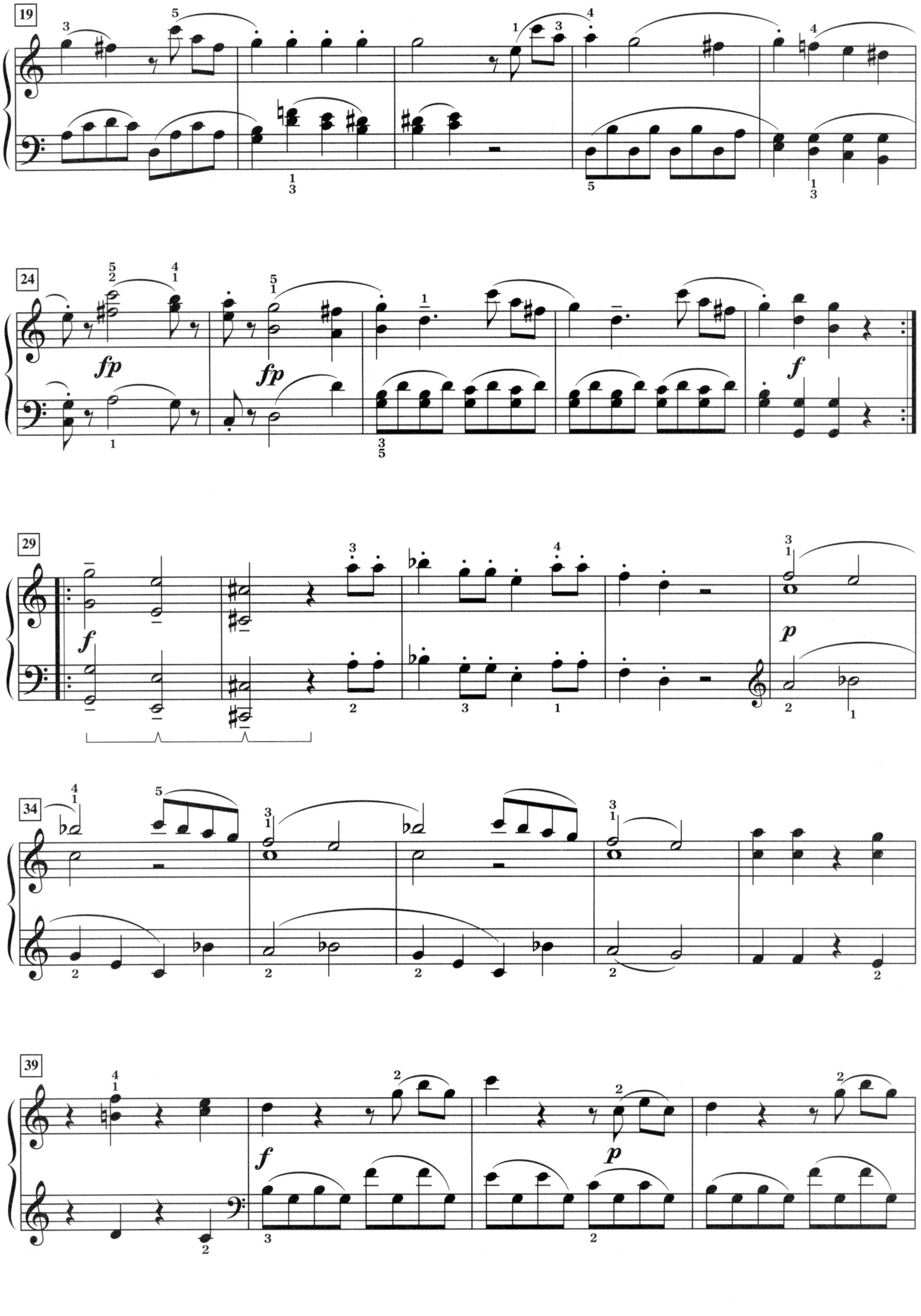
19
24
29
34
39

Viennese Sonatina No. 2 in A Major

(first movement)

(transcribed from Five Divertimenti, K. 439b)

Wolfgang Amadeus Mozart

ⓐ Arpeggiated chords should be played on the beat.

17
simile
21
25
29
33

Viennese Sonatina No. 6 in C Major

(first movement)

(transcribed from Five Divertimenti, K. 439b)

Wolfgang Amadeus Mozart

25
30
34
38
44

49
54
sf
sf
f
p
59
64
f
68
p
f
p
f

Viennese Sonatina No. 6 in C Major

(third movement)

(transcribed from Five Divertimenti, K. 439b)

Wolfgang Amadeus Mozart

cresc.

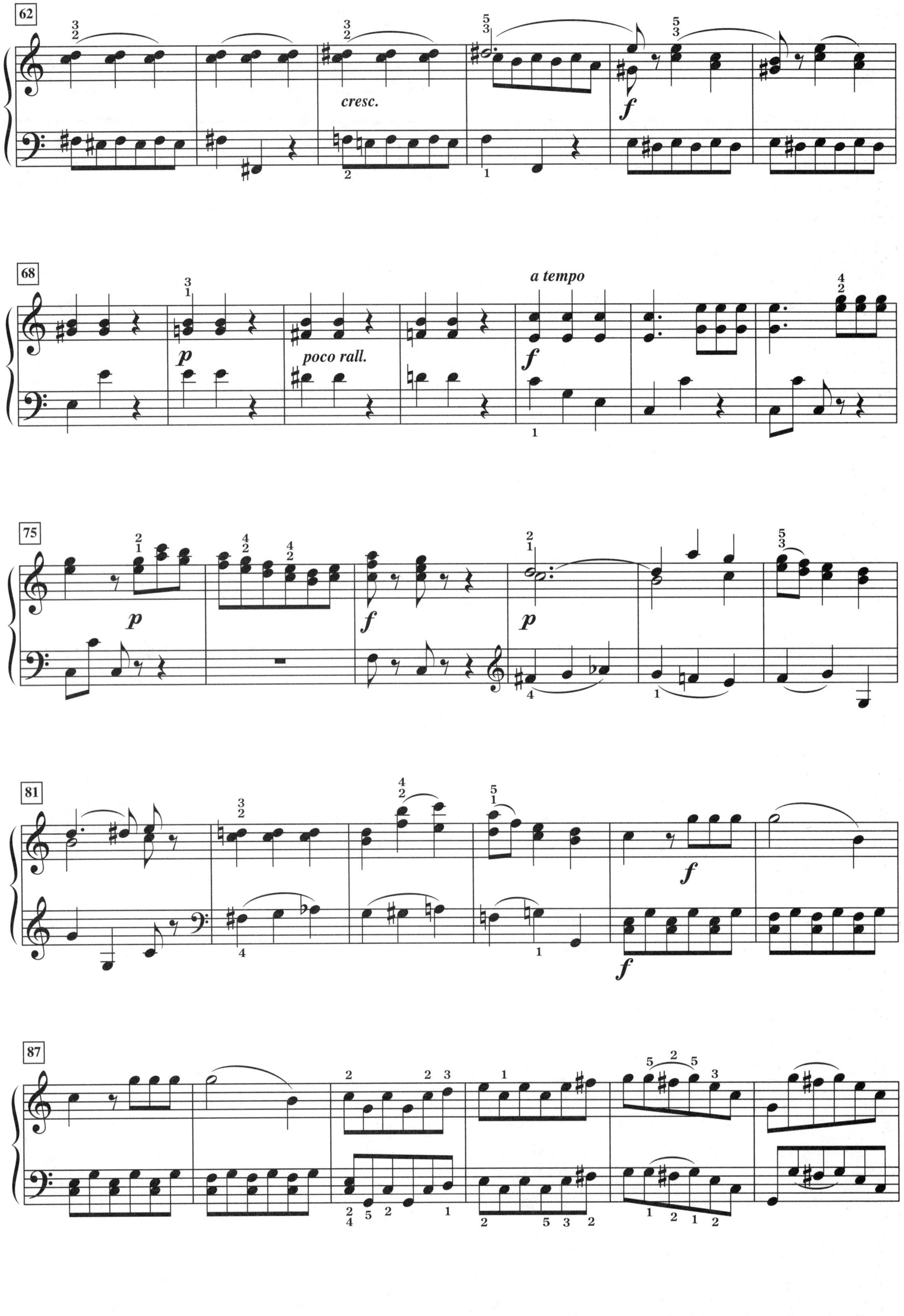
62
cresc.
68
a tempo
poco rall.
75
81
87

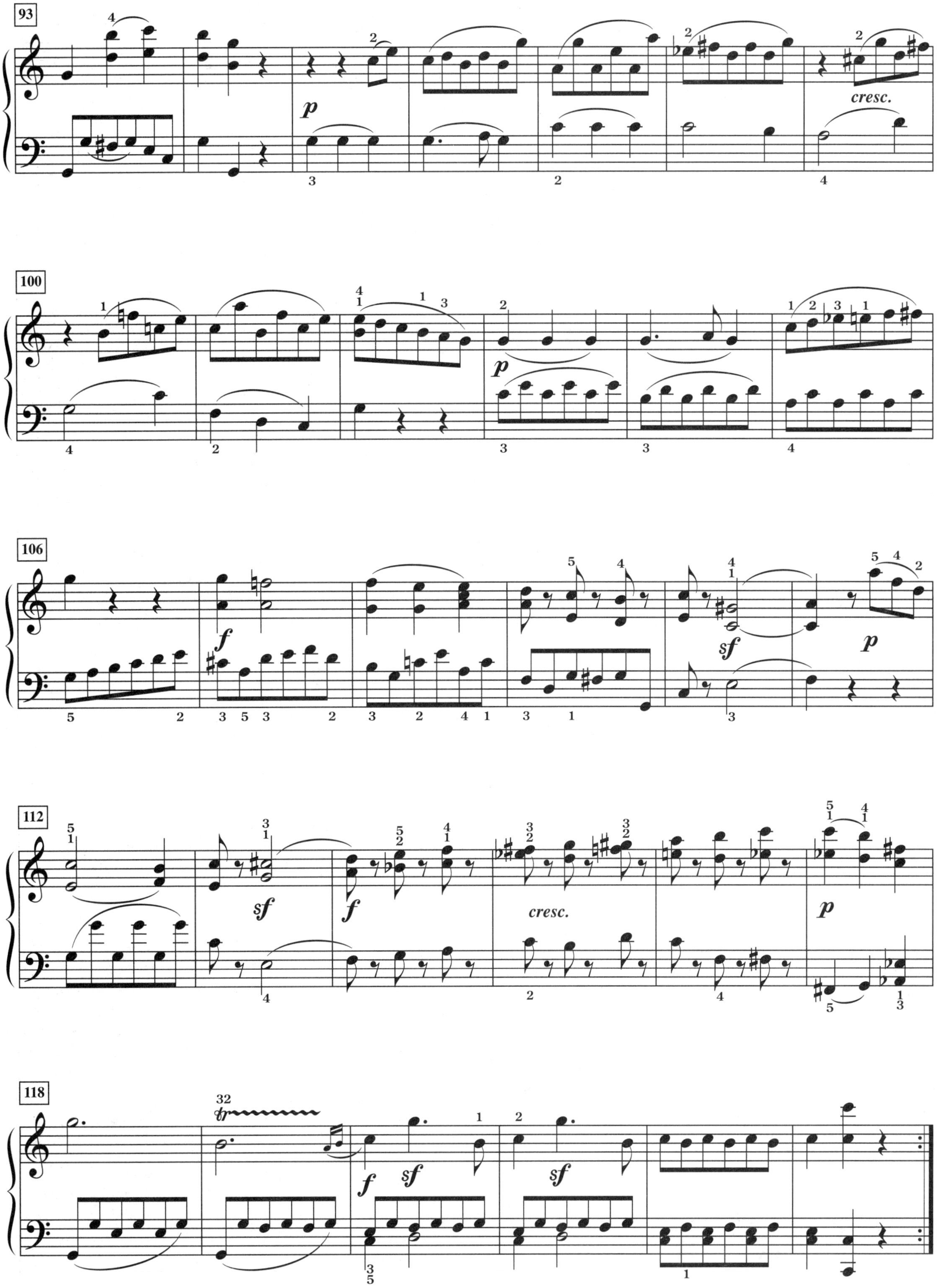
93
p
cresc.
100
p
106
f
sf
p
112
sf
f
cresc.
p
118
f
sf
sf

Sonatina in G Major

Hob. XVI: 8

(first movement)

Franz Joseph Haydn

Allegro

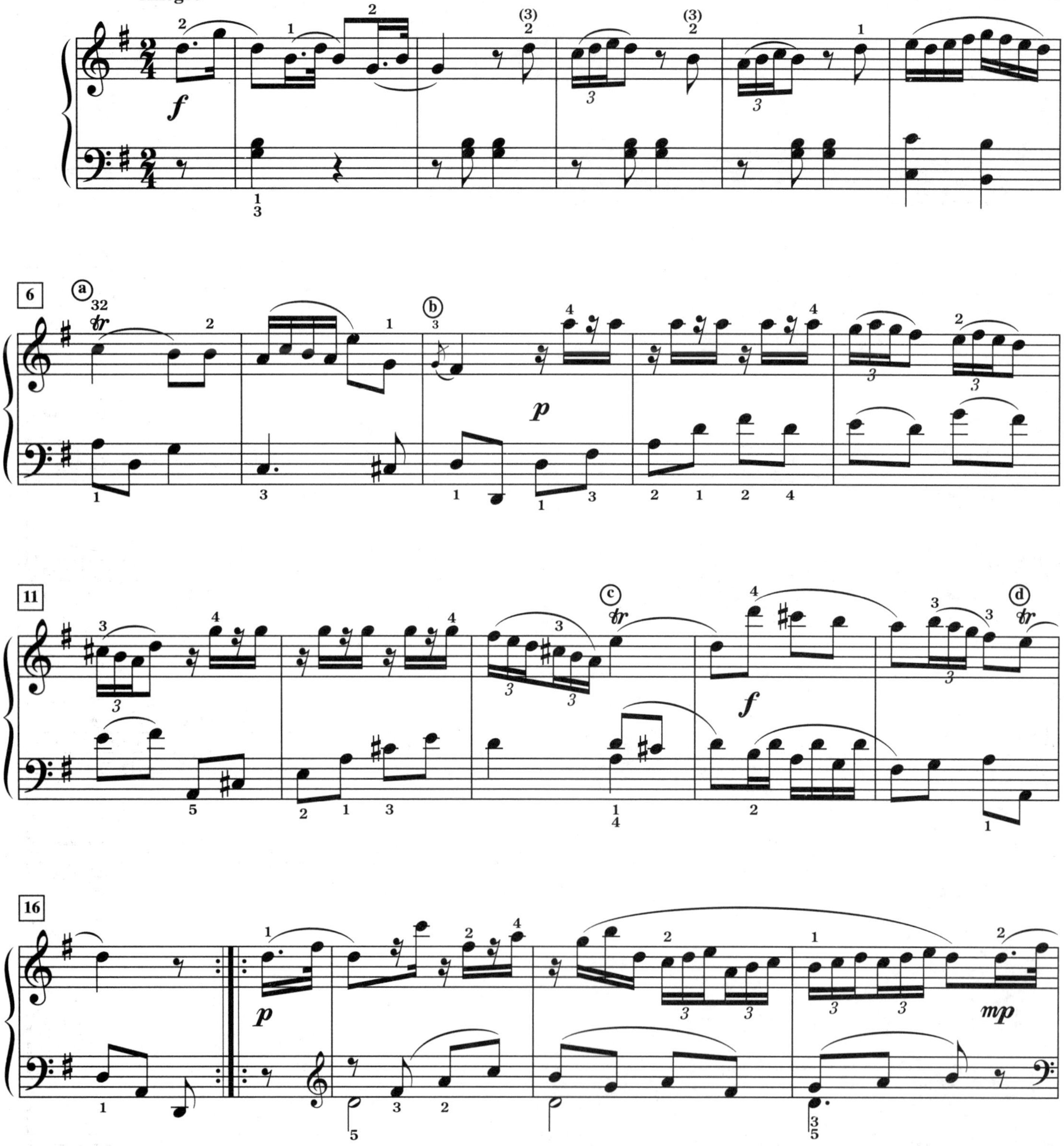

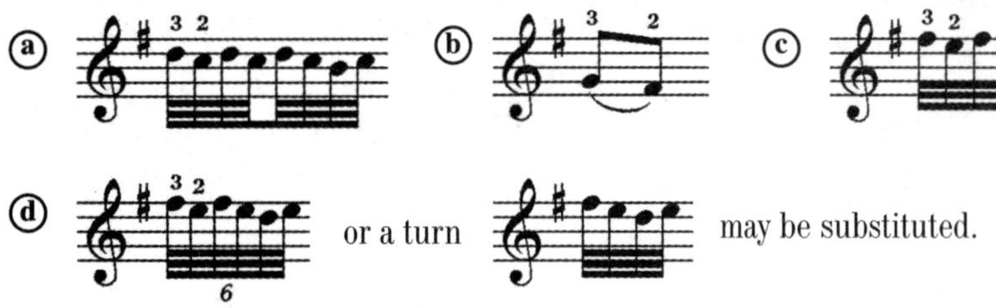
a
b
c
d
or a turn
may be substituted.

(e) 

(f) 

Sonatina in F Major

Hob. XVI: 9

(first movement)

Franz Joseph Haydn

19
mp
24
29
f
mp
mf
34
38
cresc.

Sonatina in C Major

Hob. XVI: 10

(first movement)

Franz Joseph Haydn

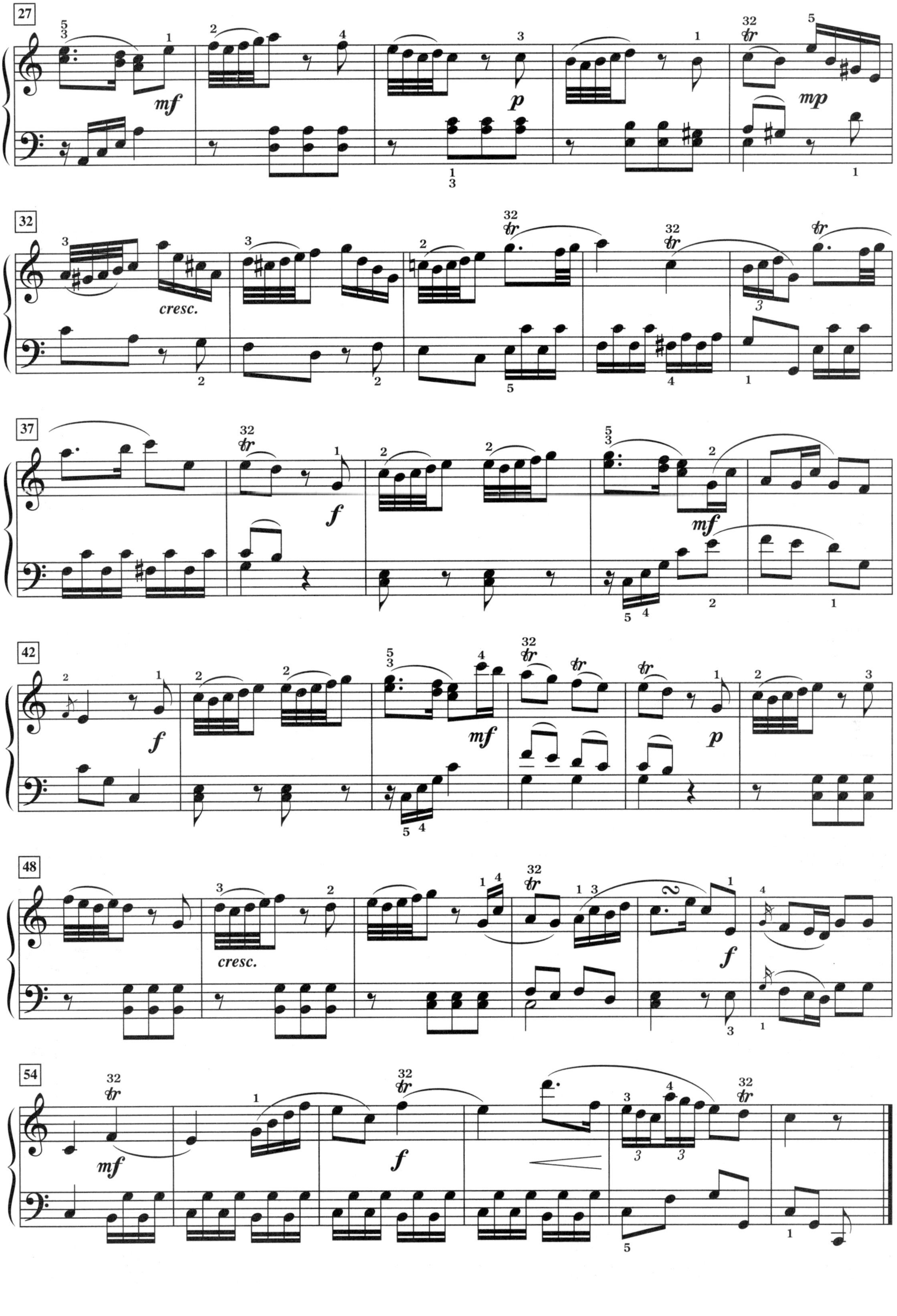
27
mf
p
mp
32
cresc.
37
f
mf
42
f
mf
p
48
cresc.
f
54
mf
f

Bagatelle in G Minor

Op. 119, No. 1

Ludwig van Beethoven

Allegretto

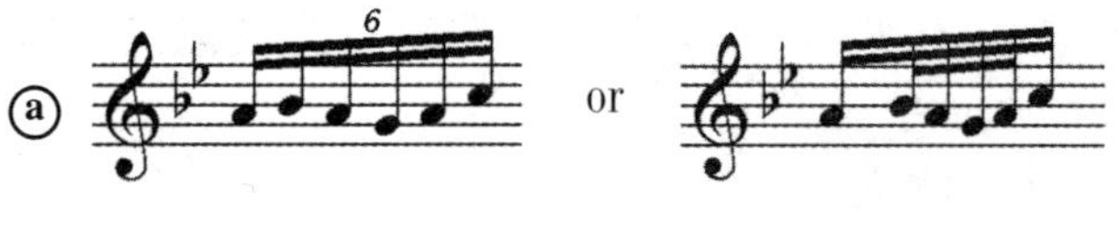

23
1.
2.
28
1.
34
2.
mp
poco rit.
39
a tempo
p
45

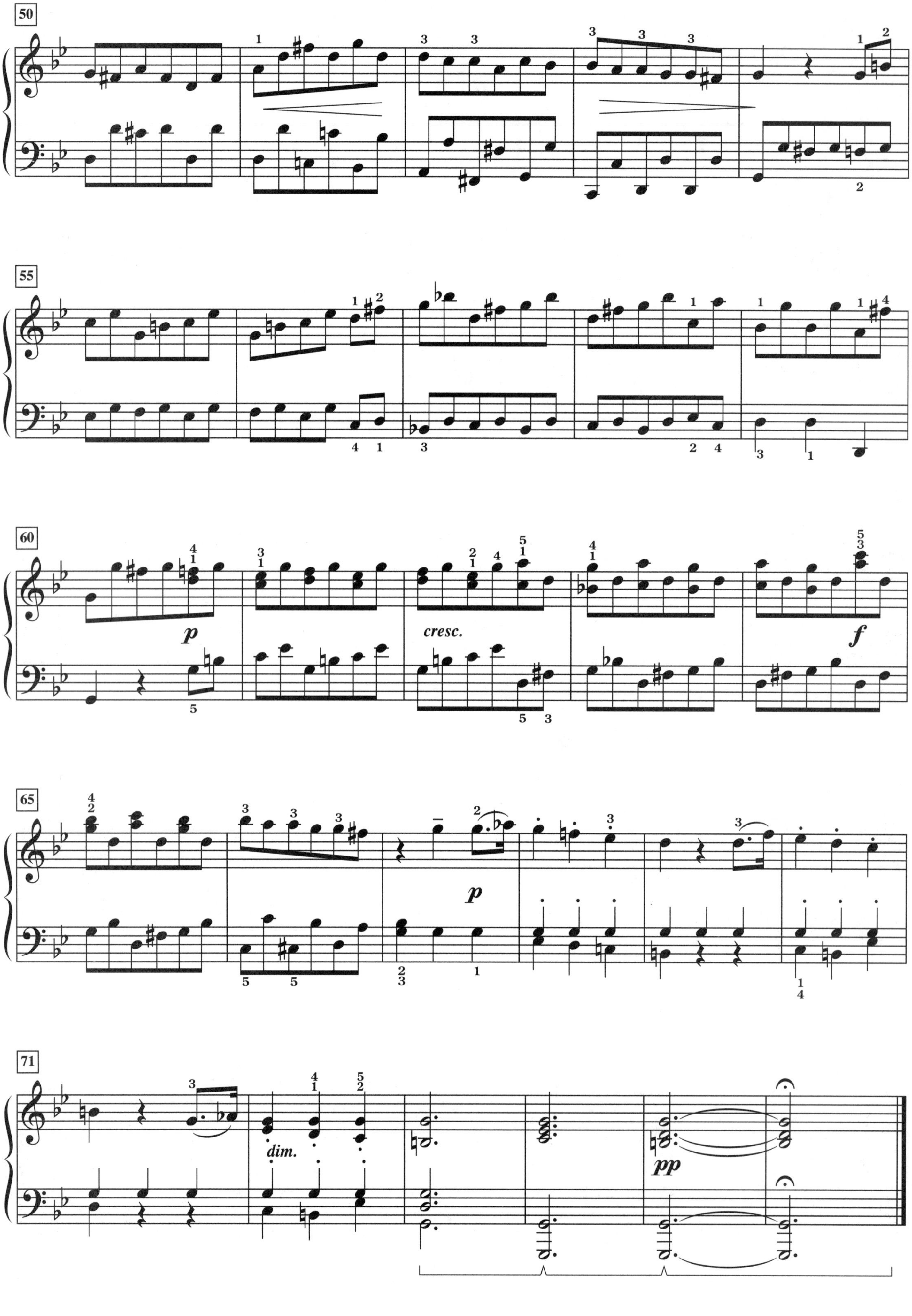
50
55
60
p
cresc.
f
65
p
71
dim.
pp

Bagatelle in A Minor

Op. 119, No. 9

Ludwig van Beethoven

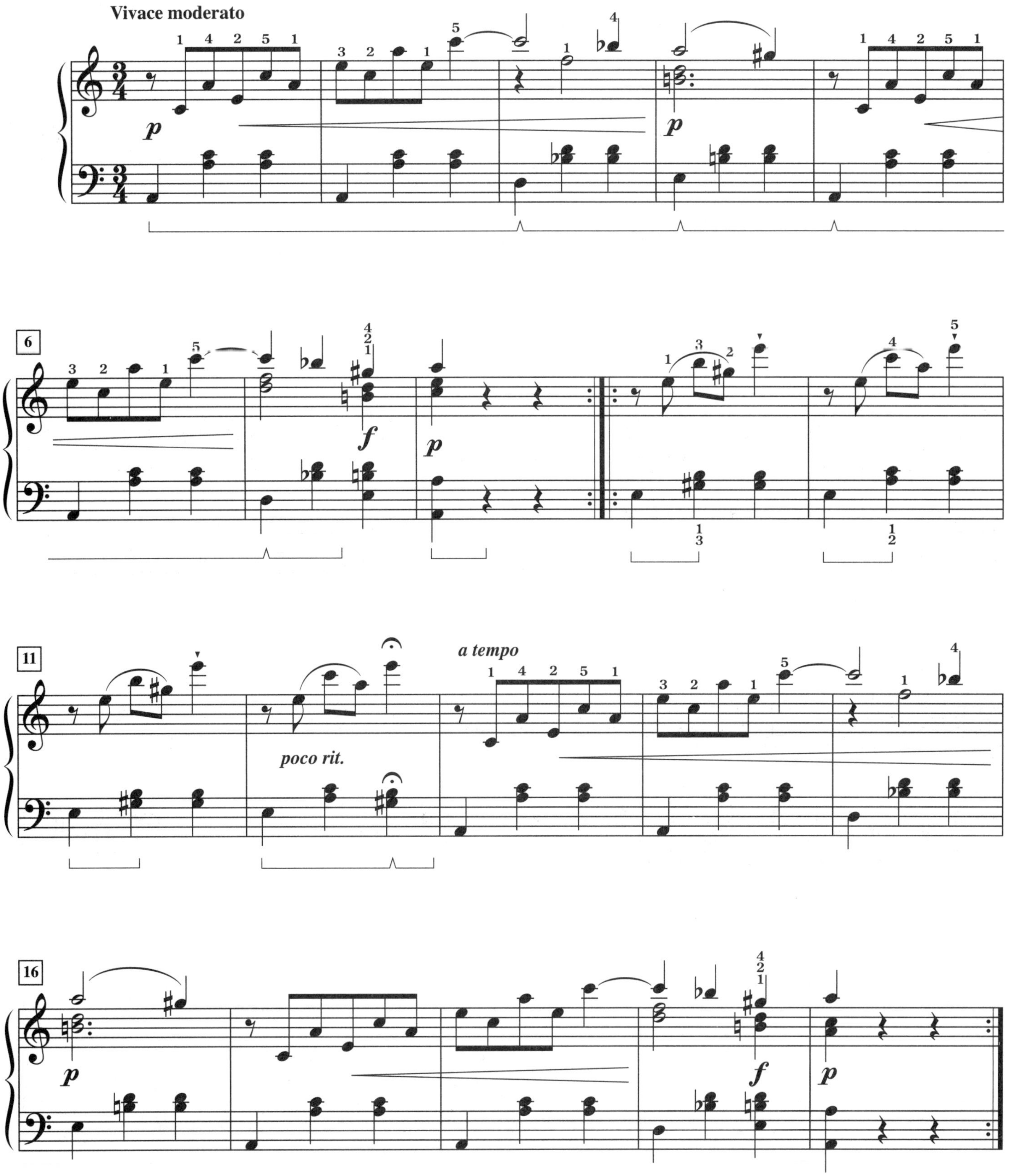

Bagatelle in D Major

Op. 119, No. 3

Ludwig van Beethoven

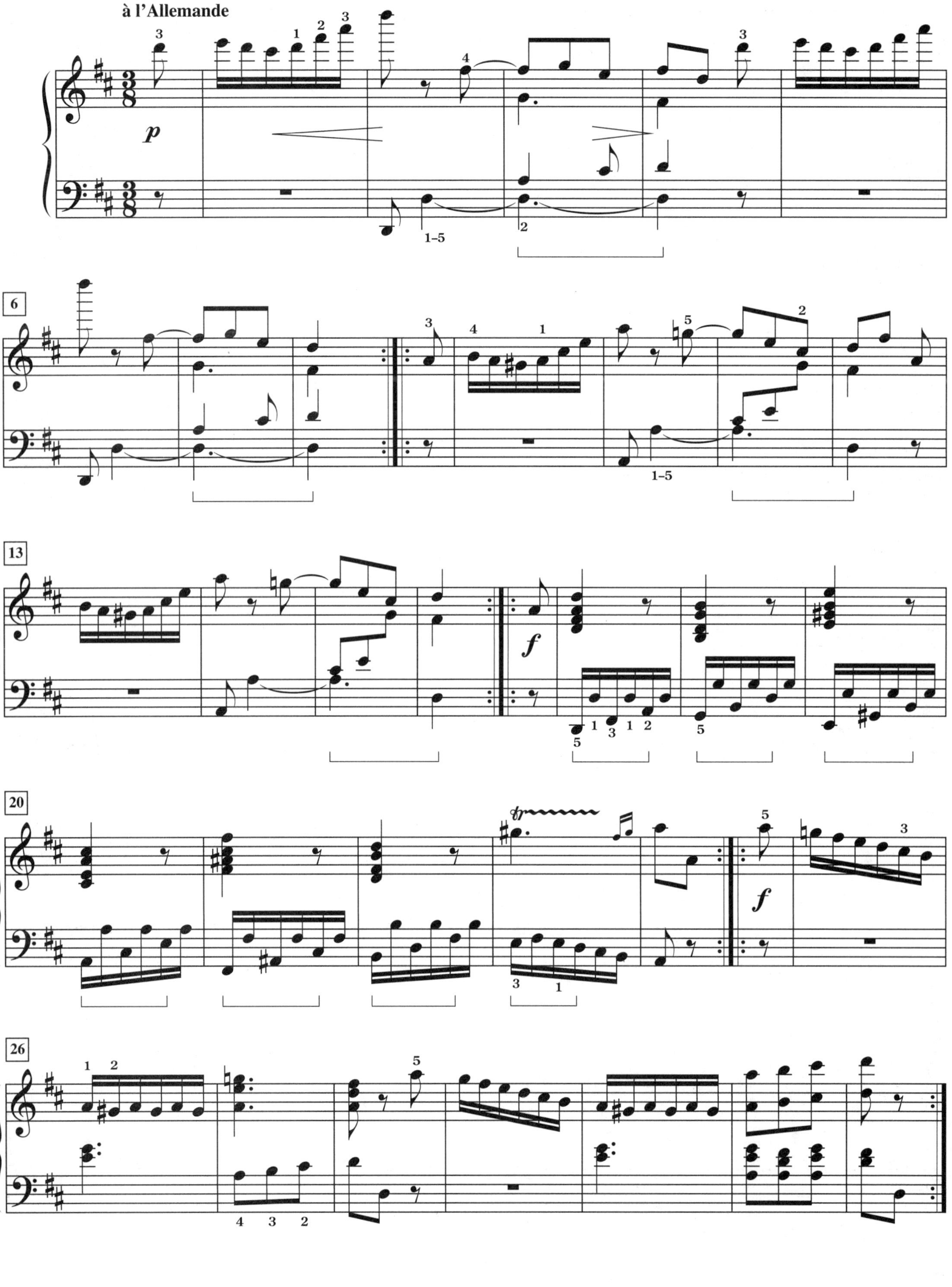

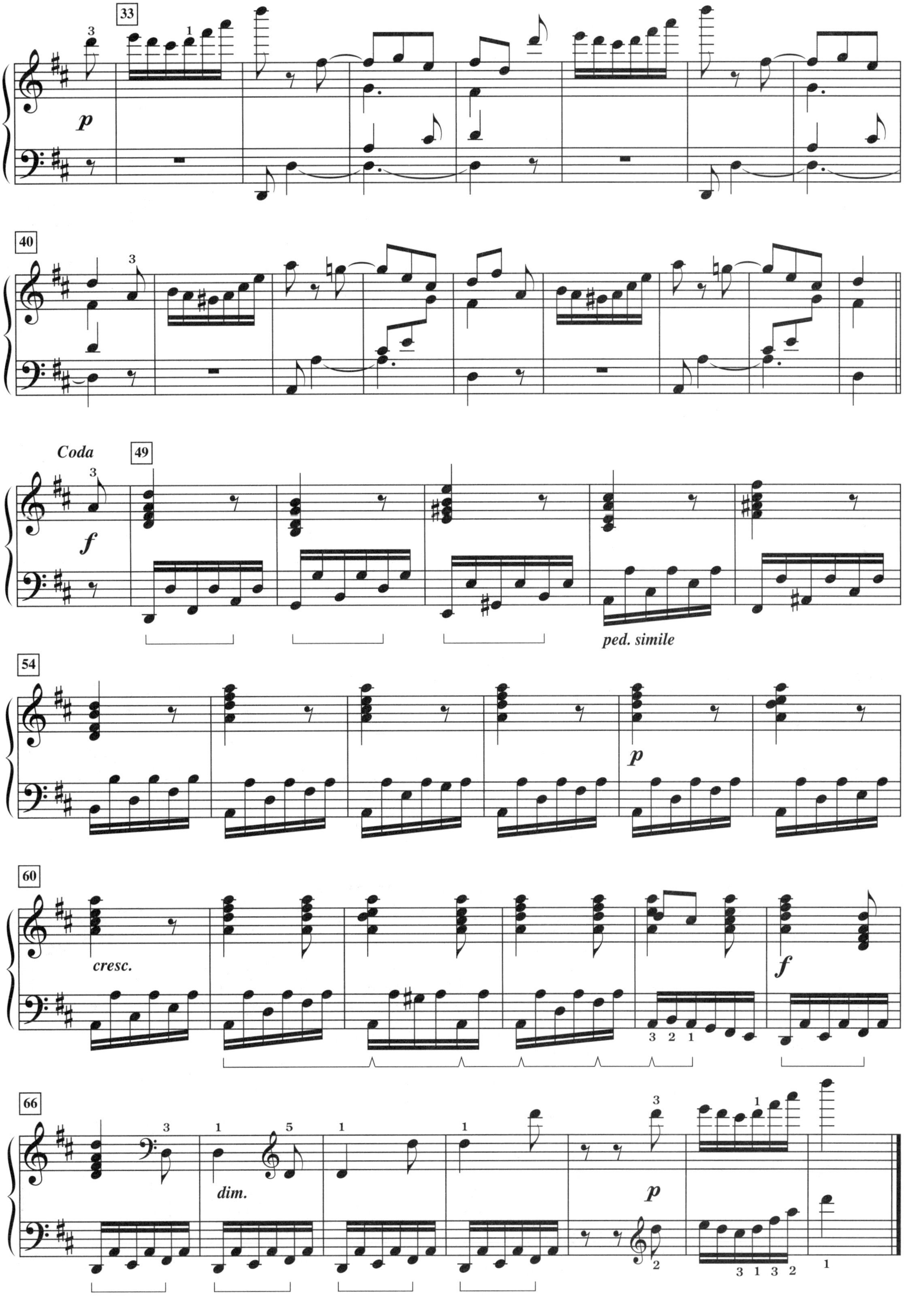
33
p
40
Coda
49
f
ped. simile
54
p
60
cresc.
f
66
dim.
p

Six Variations on a Swiss Folk Song

WoO 64

Ludwig van Beethoven

Andante con moto

Theme

ⓐ Italicized fingering by Beethoven.

Var. II
23
f
26
30
Var. III
Minore
34
sempre p e legato
38
simile
42

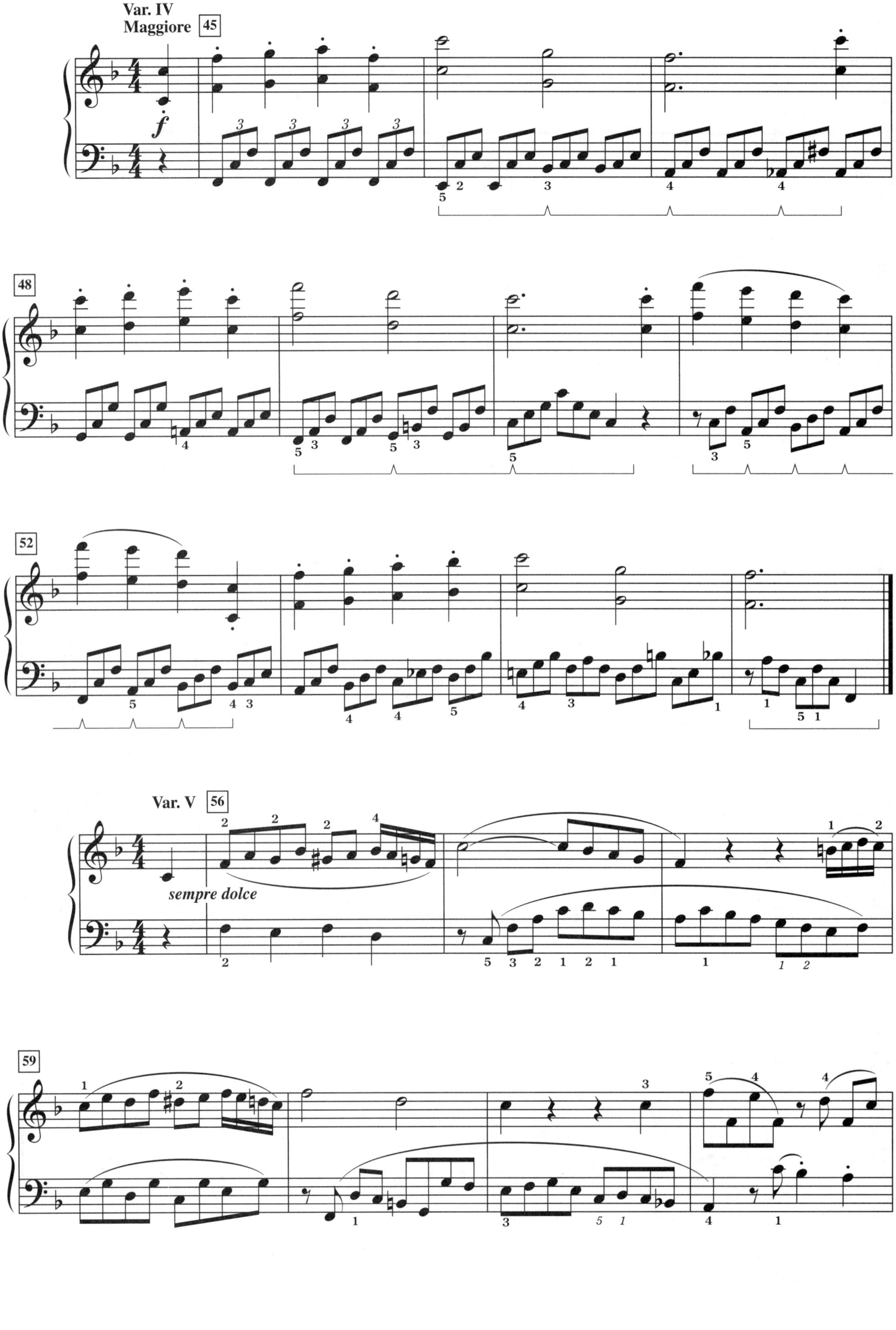
Var. IV
Maggiore
45
48
52
Var. V
56
sempre dolce
59

63
Var. VI
67
70
73
76
Coda

German Dance in D Major

D. 783, No. 2

Franz Schubert

Waltz in B Minor

D. 145, No. 6

Franz Schubert

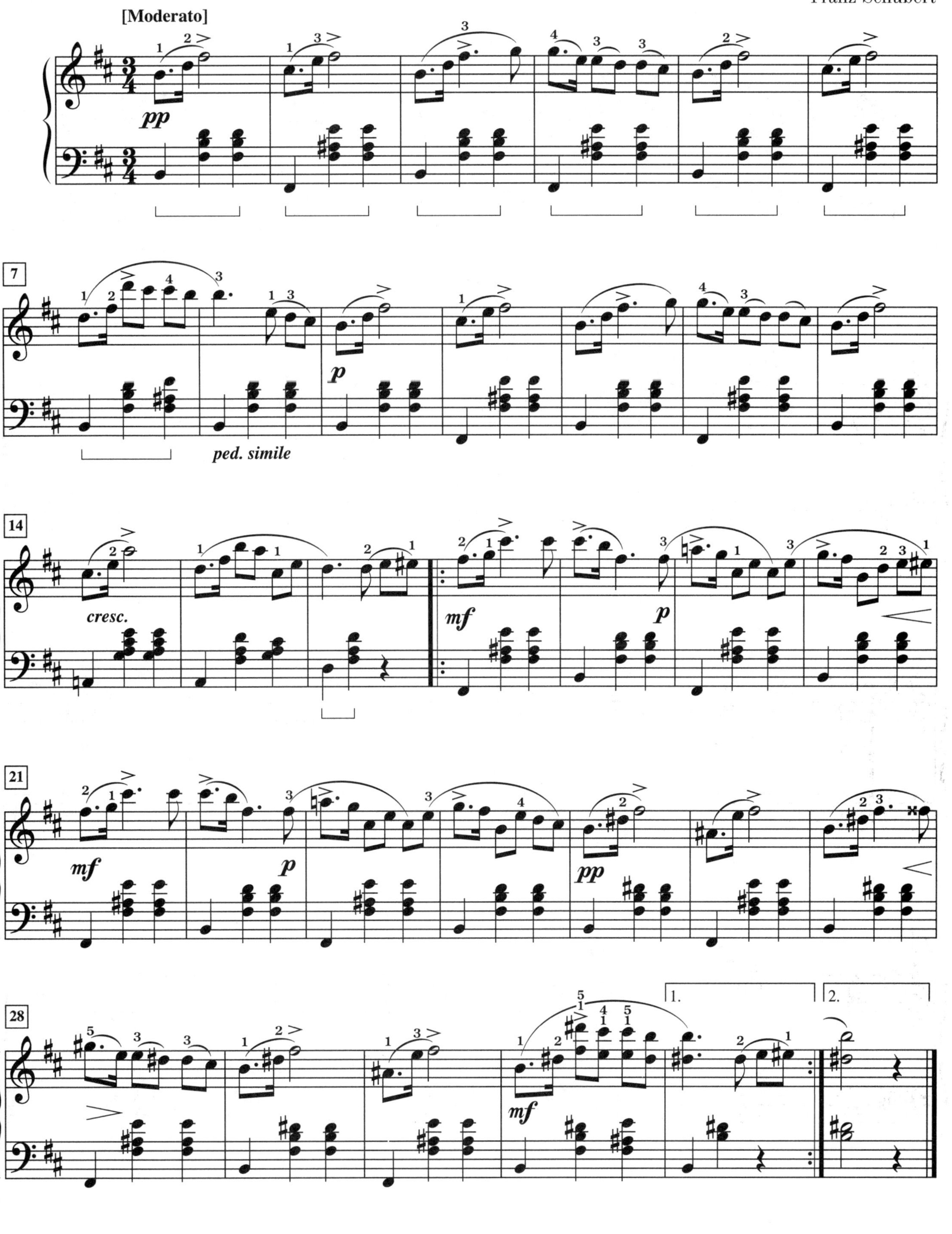

Waltz in A-flat Major

D. 365, No. 2

Franz Schubert

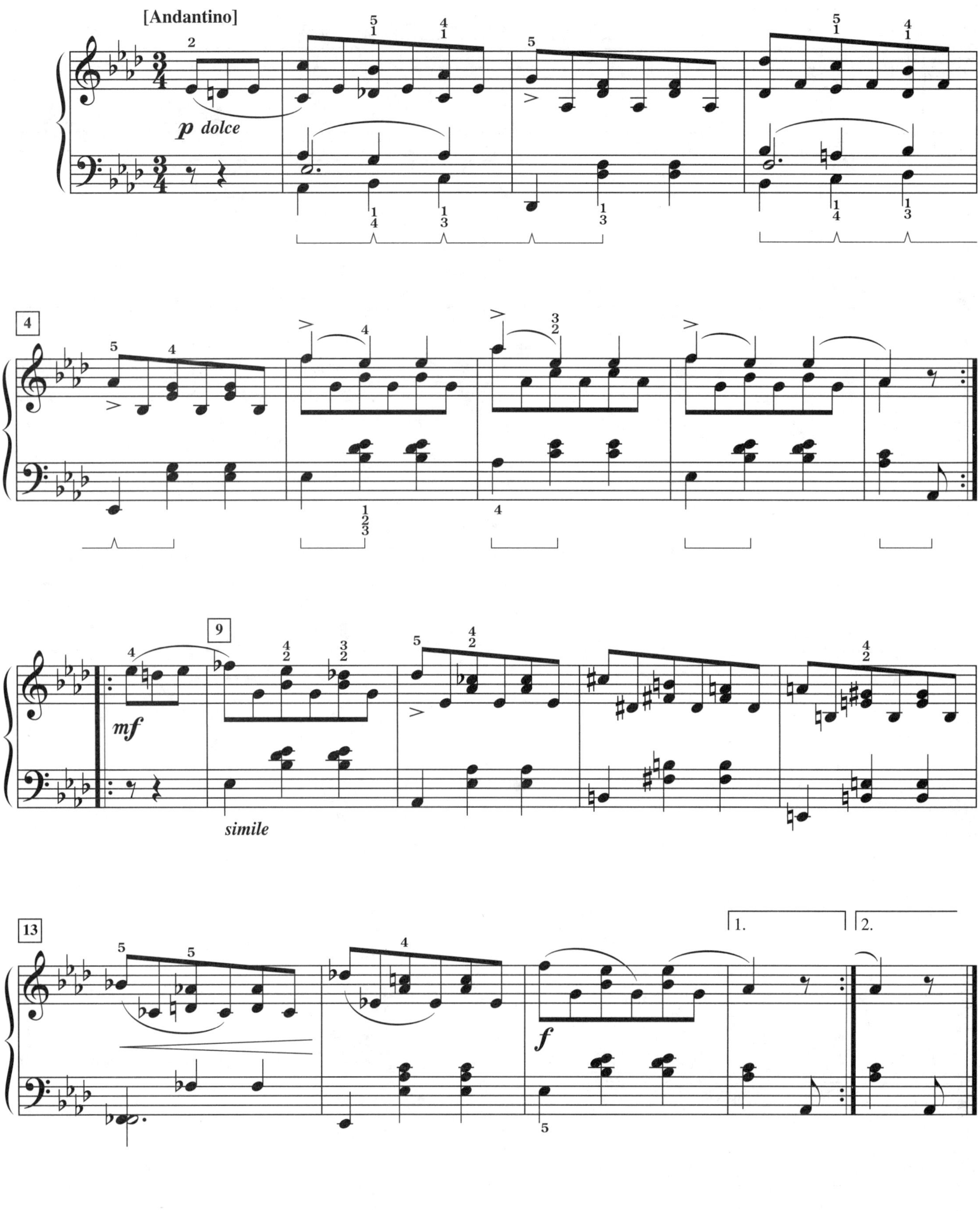

Two Ecossaises

D. 421, Nos. 1 and 2

Franz Schubert

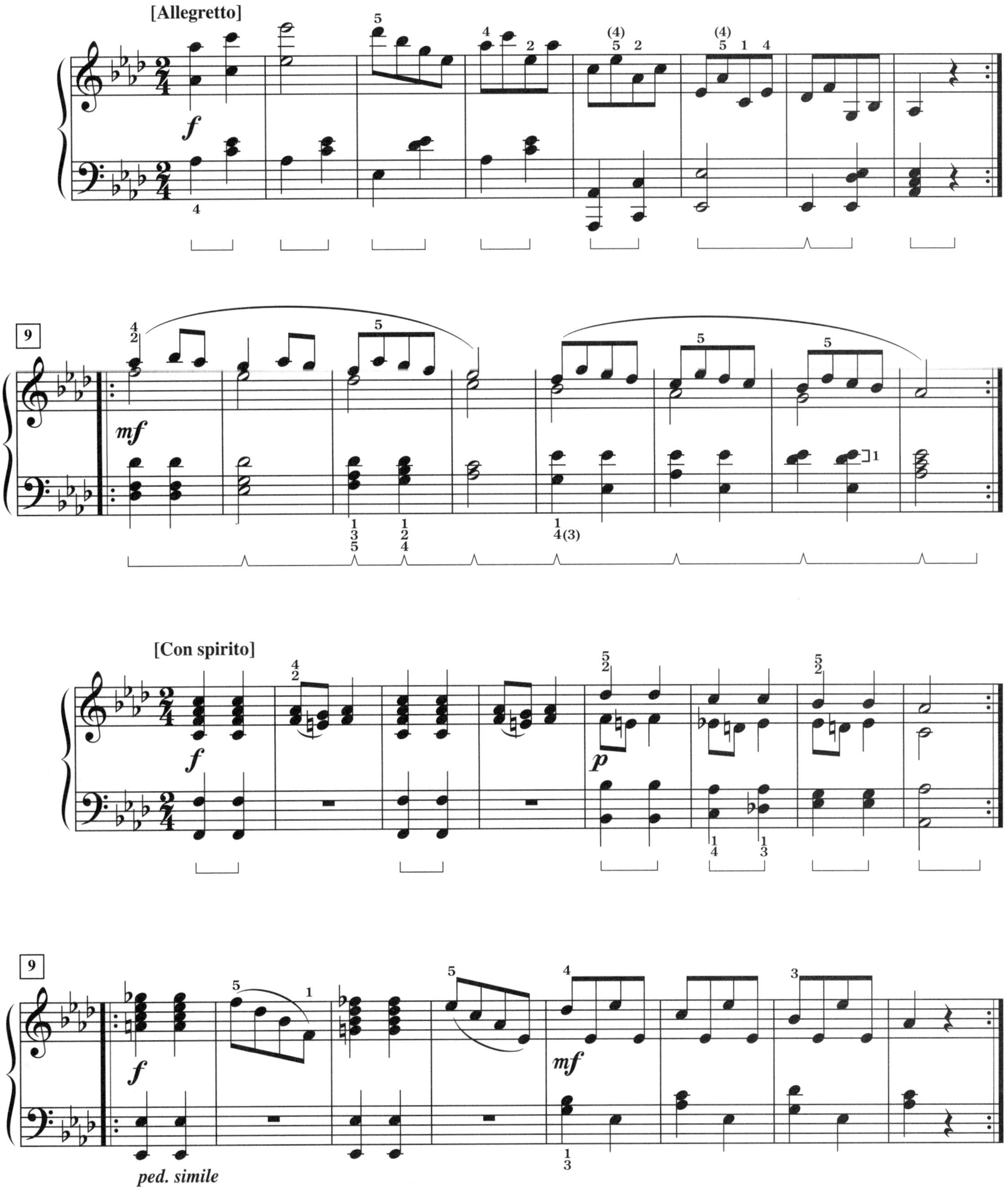

Album Leaf in F-sharp Minor

Op. 99, No. 4

Robert Schumann

Ziemlich langsam (quite slowly)

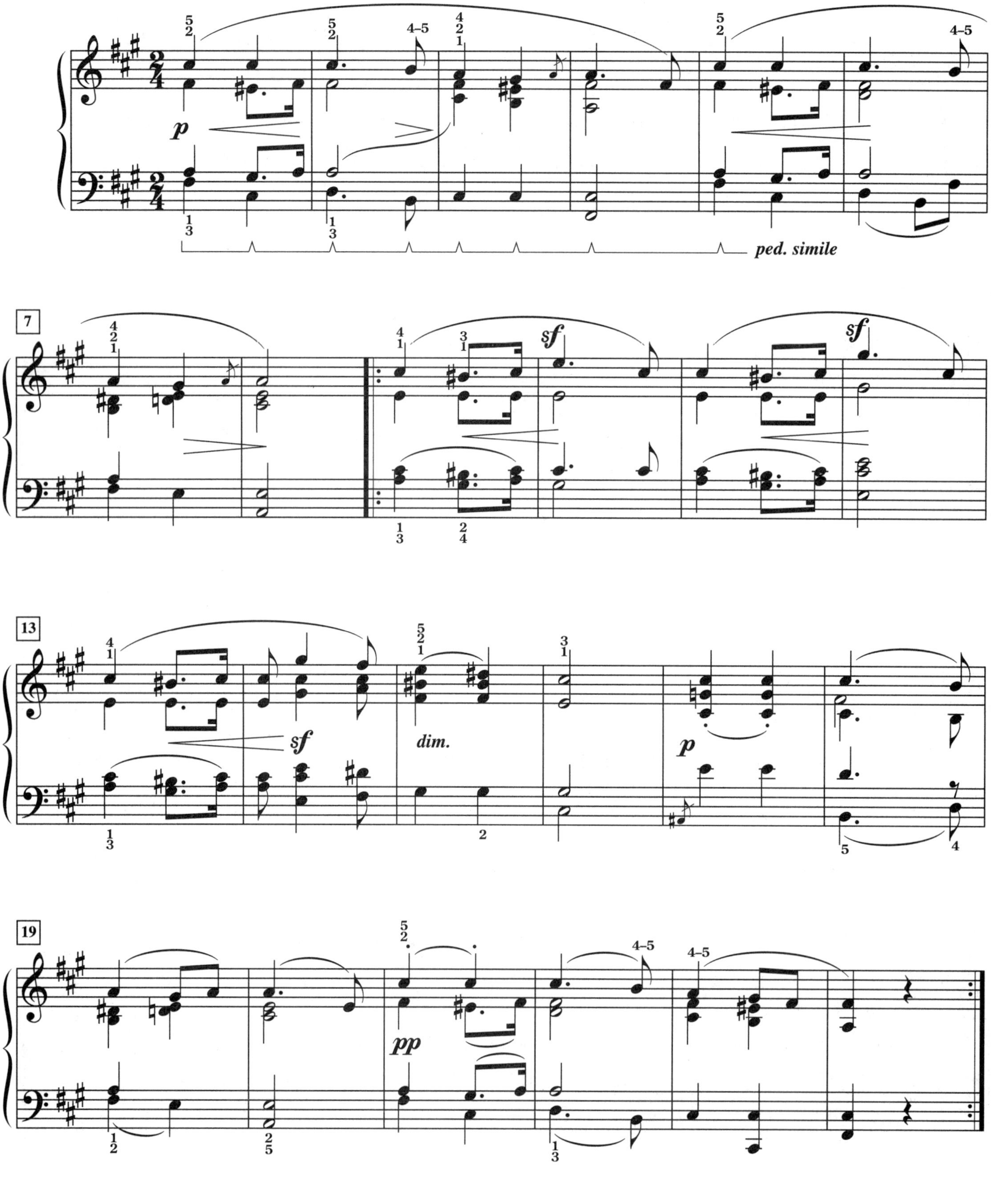

From Foreign Lands and Places

Op. 15, No. 1

Robert Schumann

Mignon

Op. 68, No. 35

Robert Schumann

Langsam, zart
(Slowly, tenderly)

ⓐ The Clara Schumann edition adds a footnote: "The ***fp*** is to be understood merely as a slight emphasis on the last quarter note."

13
sf
sf
17
p
cresc.
21
pp
25
pp
29
1.
2.
dim.
rit.

Important Event

Op. 15, No. 6

Robert Schumann

Prelude in A Major

Op. 28, No. 7

Frédéric Chopin

Mazurka in F Major

Op. 68, No. 3

Frédéric Chopin

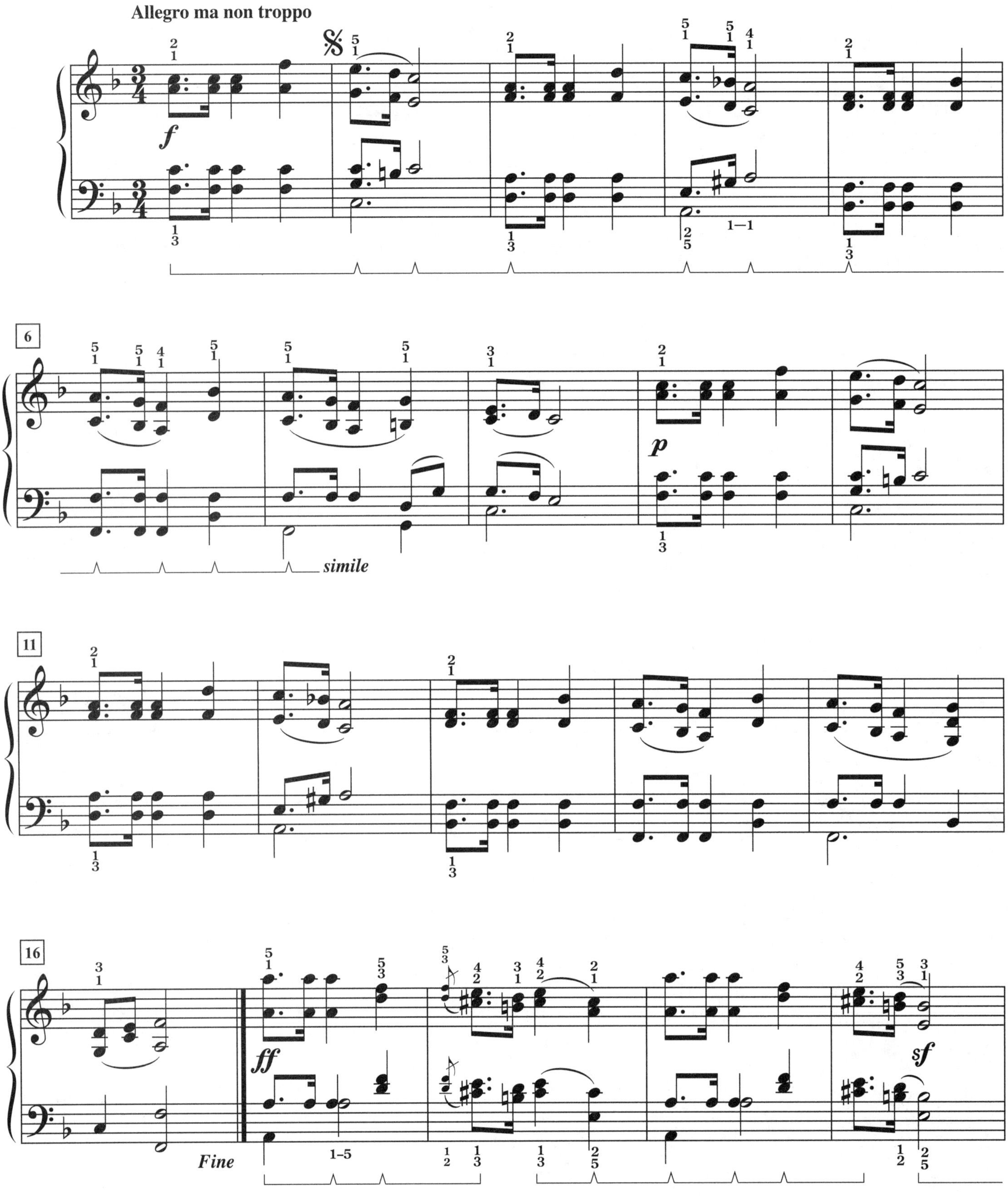

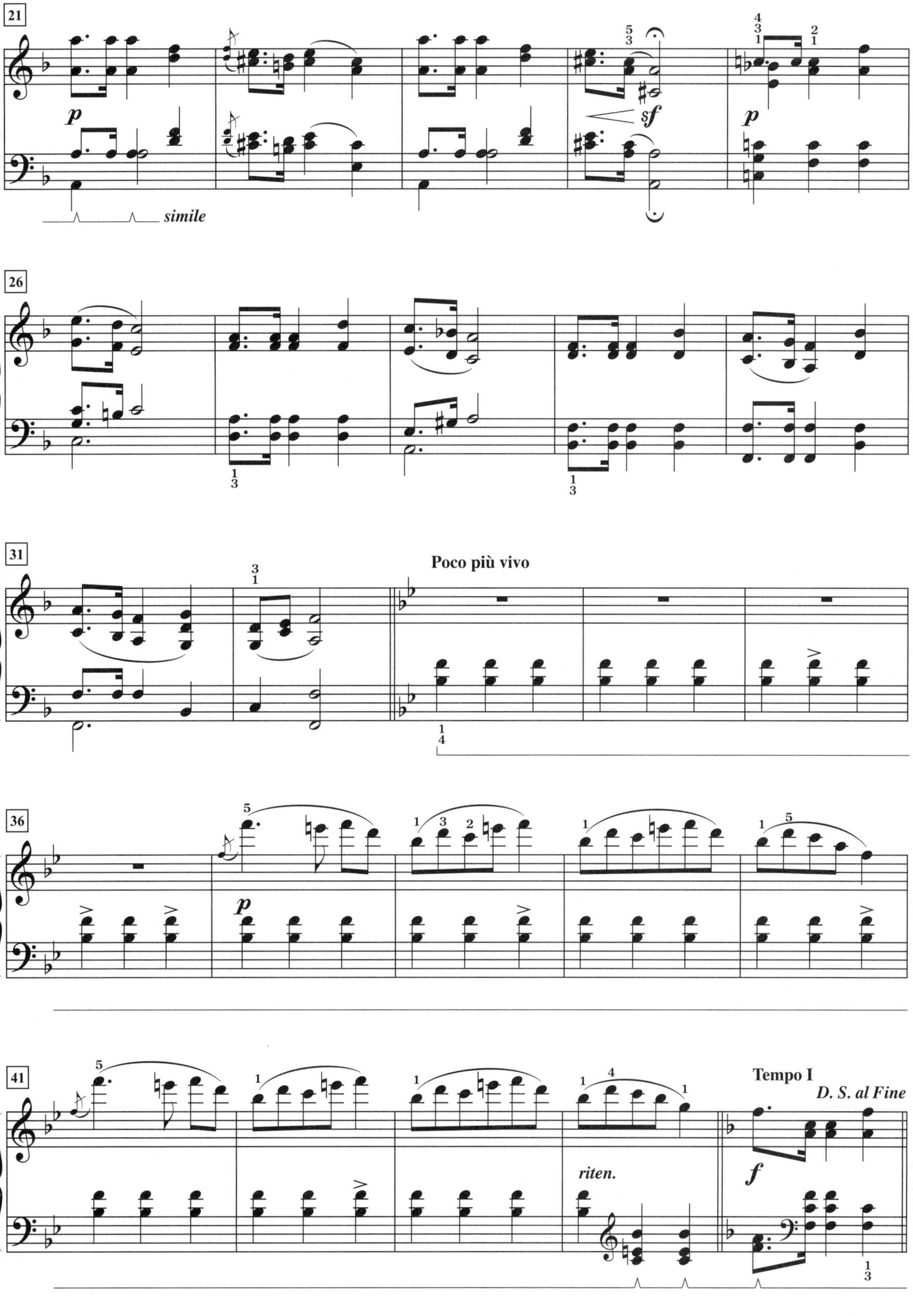
21
p
simile
sf
p
26
31
Poco più vivo
36
p
41
riten.
Tempo I
D. S. al Fine
f

Mazurka in G Minor

Op. 67, No. 2

Frédéric Chopin

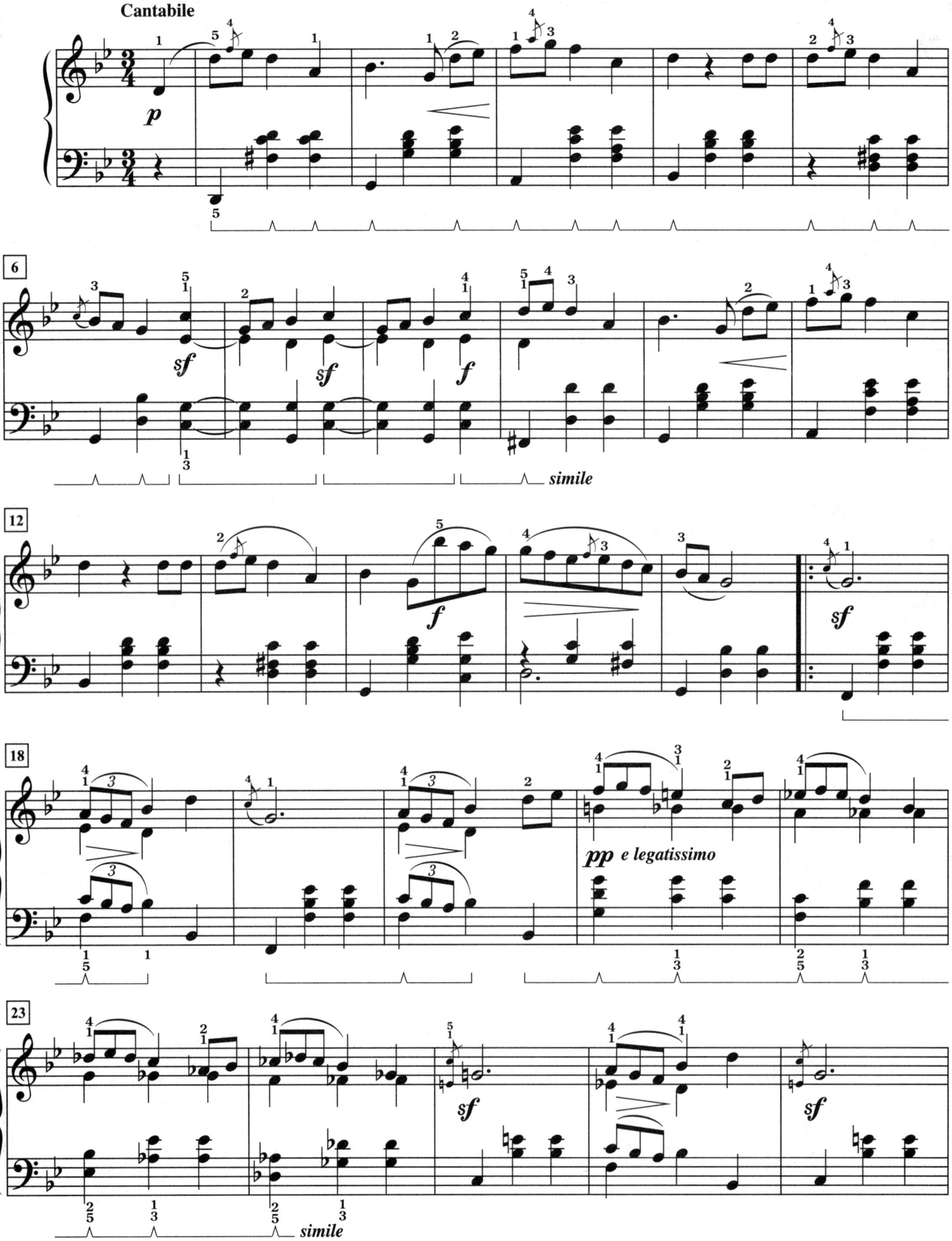

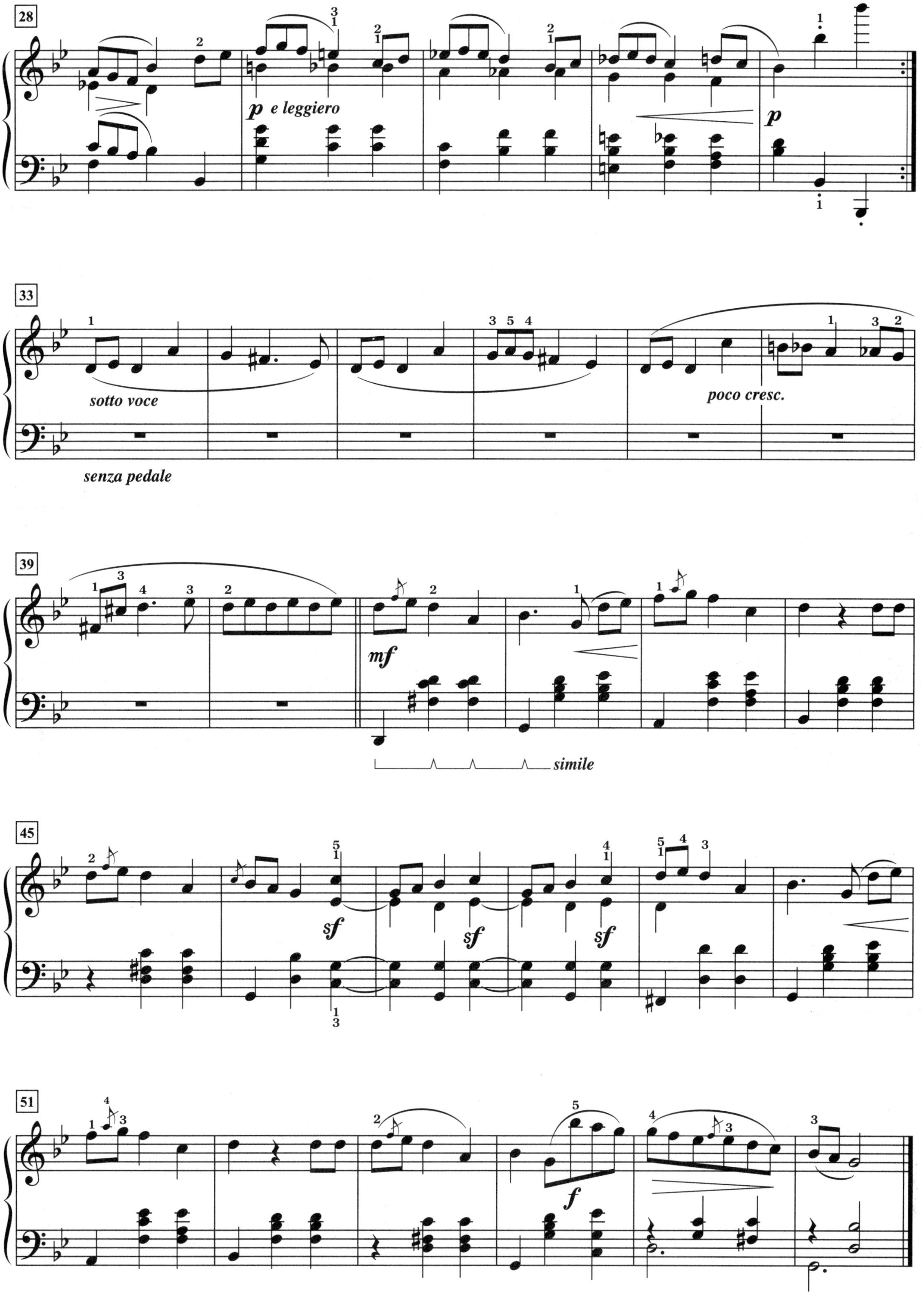
28
p e leggiero
p
33
sotto voce
poco cresc.
senza pedale
39
mf
simile
45
sf
sf
sf
51
f

Mazurka in G Major

Op. Post.

Frédéric Chopin

ⓐ 

ⓑ Measures 1–8, 9–16 and 1–8 follow here, then the Trio followed by measures 1–8 one final time.

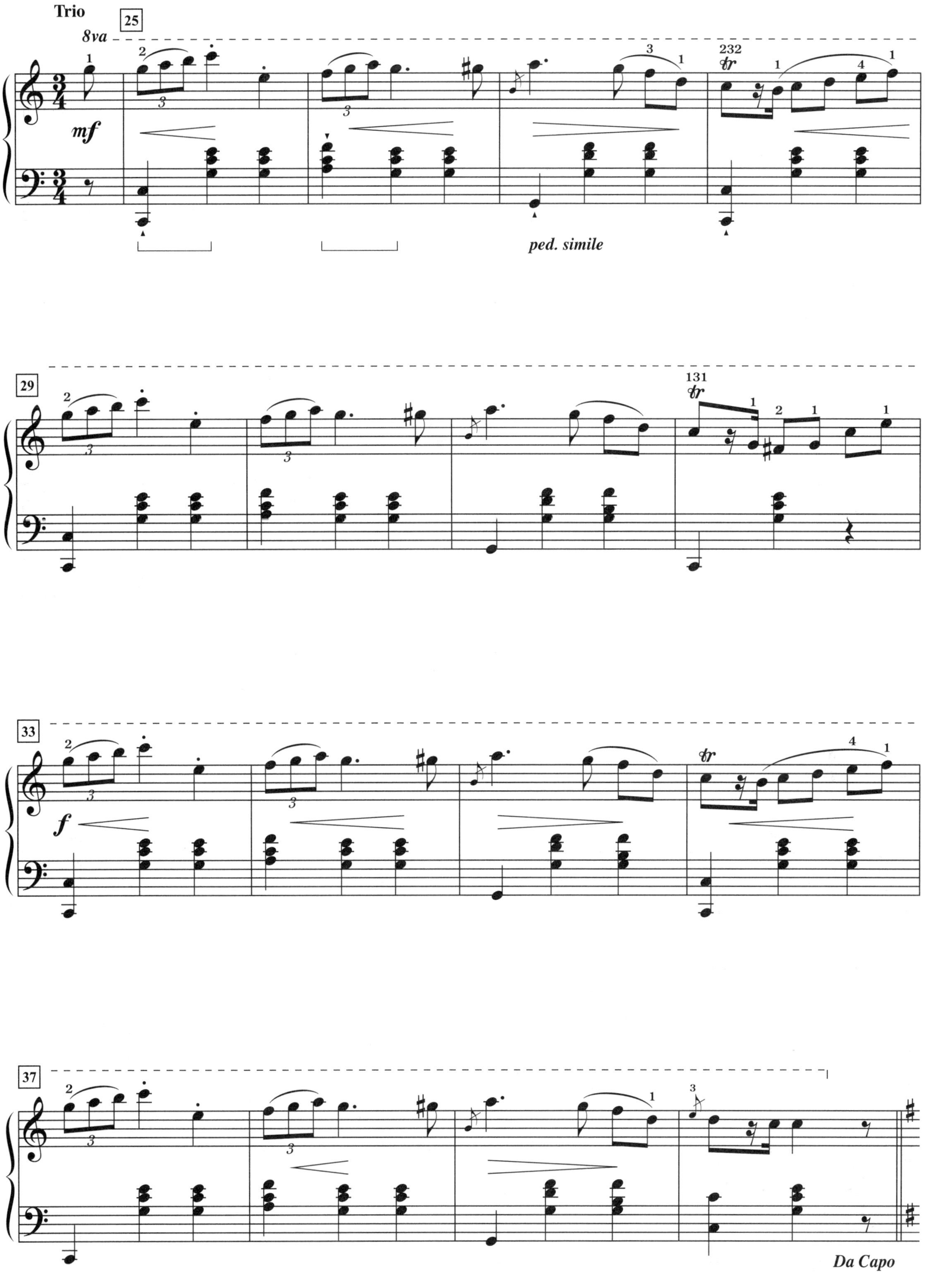
Trio
25
8va
mf
ped. simile
29
33
f
37
Da Capo

Mazurka in B-flat Major

Op. Post.

Frédéric Chopin

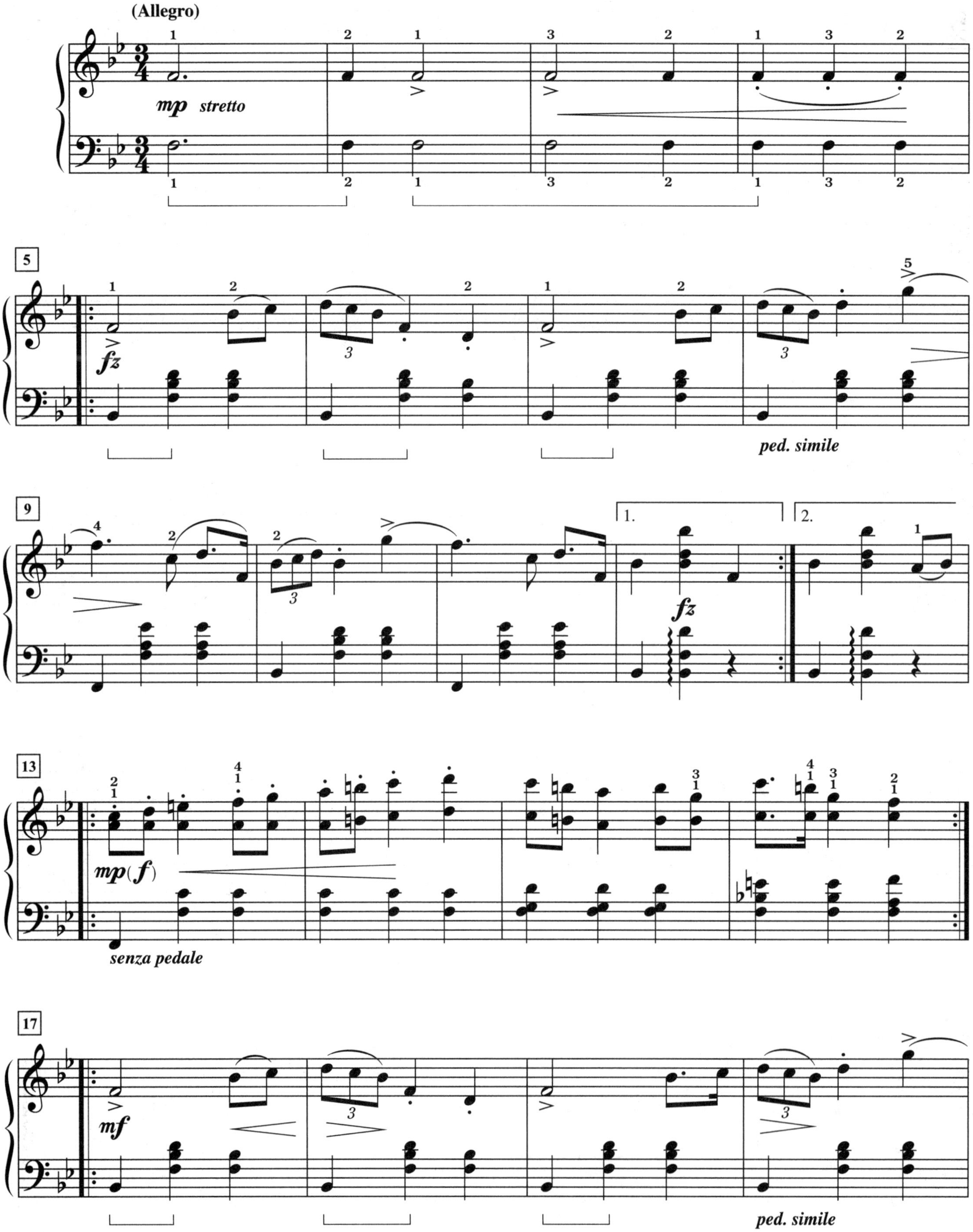

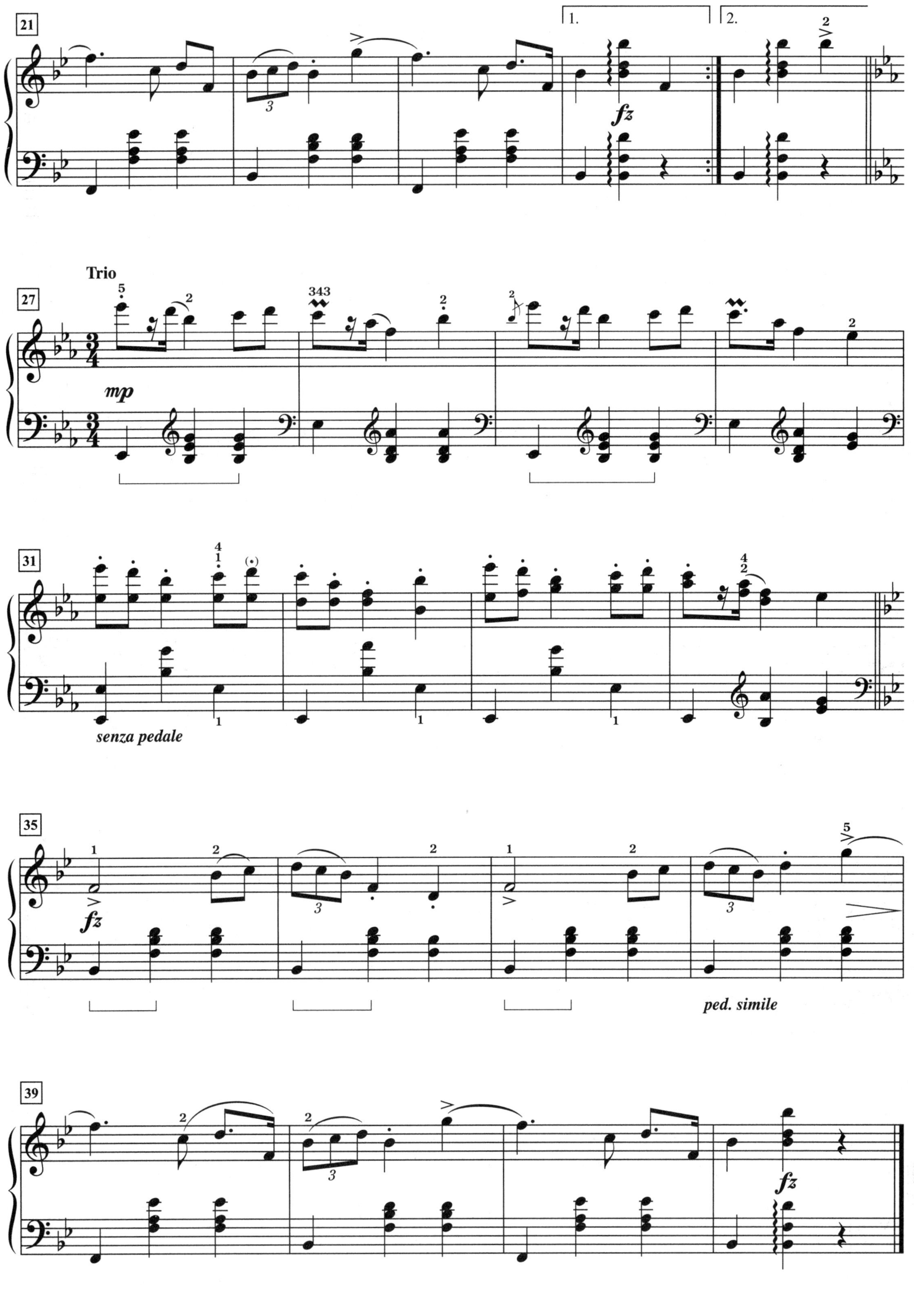
Trio
mp
senza pedale
fz
ped. simile

Waltz

Op. 38, No. 7

Edvard Grieg

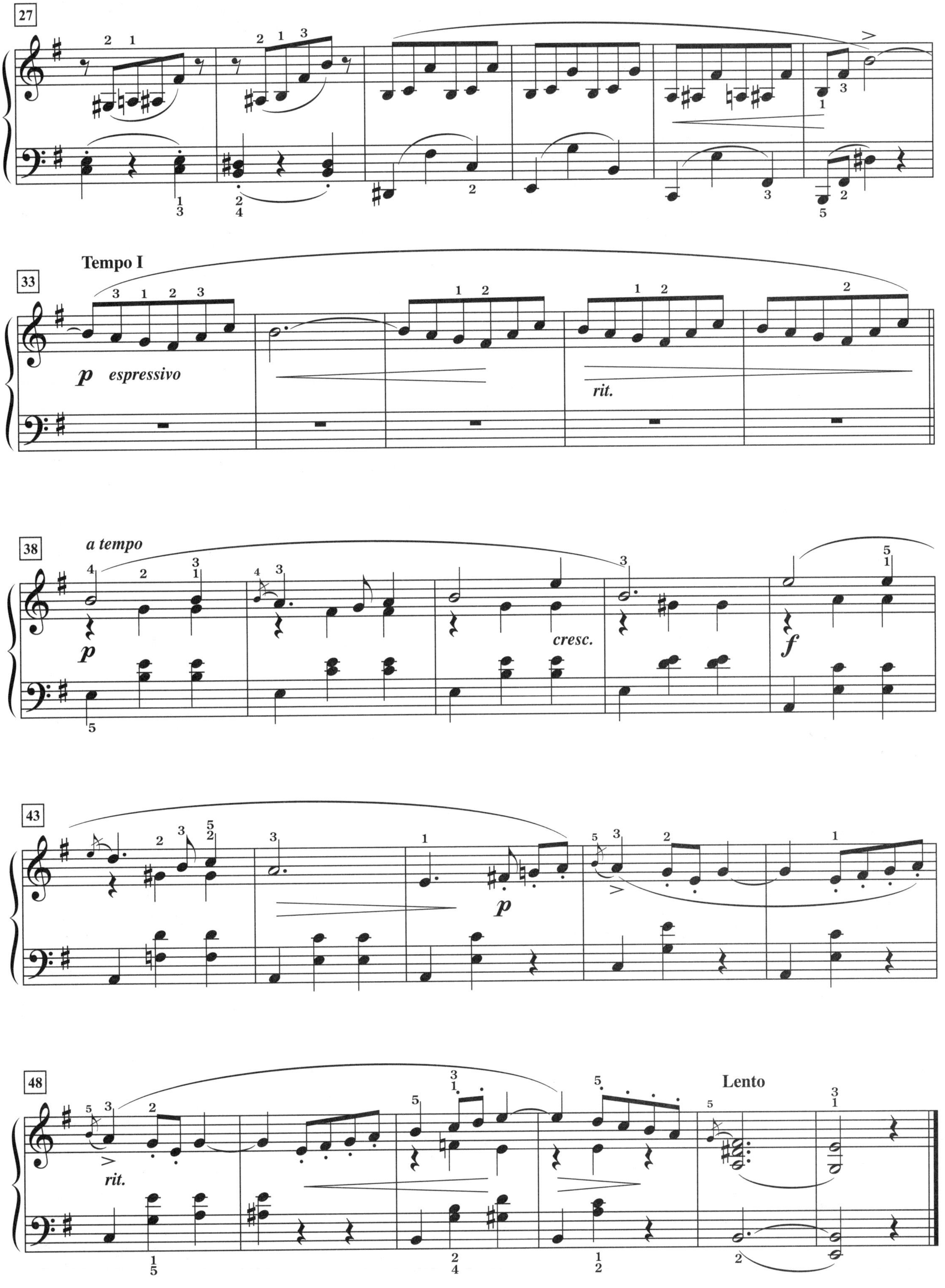

27
Tempo I
33
p espressivo
rit.
38
a tempo
p
cresc.
f
43
p
48
rit.
Lento

Norwegian Melody

Op. 12, No. 6

Presto marcato

Edvard Grieg

29
fz
fz
pp
fz
35
fz
fz
fz
fz
41
fz
fz
46
fz
fz
fz
ff
51
fz
fz sempre rit.
fz

Song of the Cowherd

Op. 17, No. 22

Edvard Grieg

The Little Shepherd

Claude Debussy

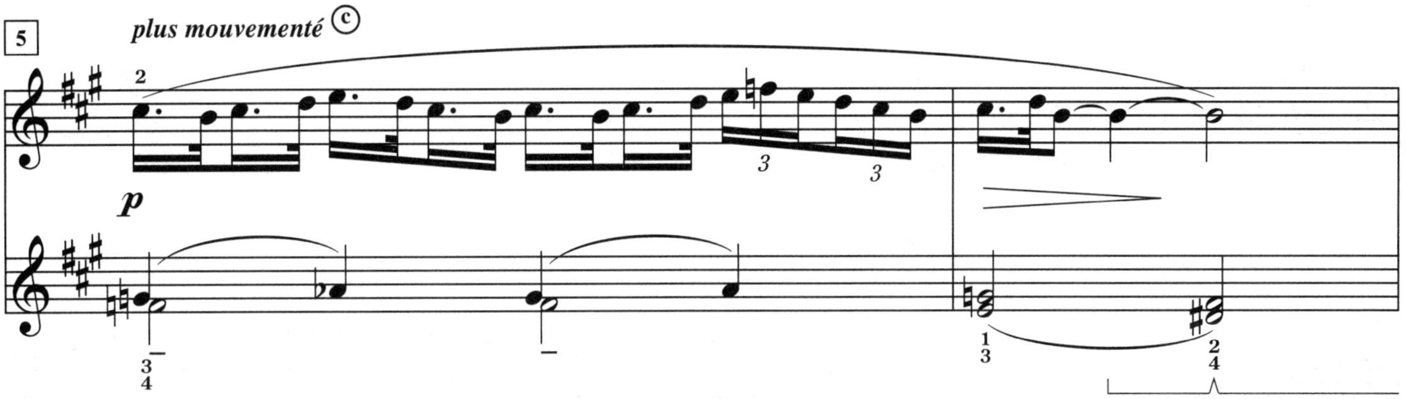

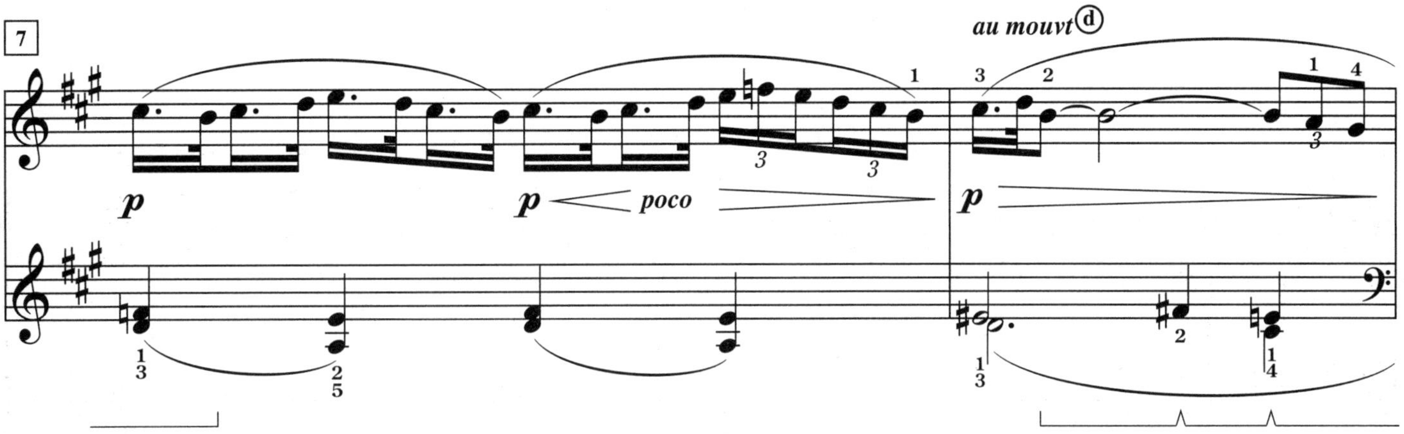

ⓐ very moderately ⓑ very sweetly and delicately expressive ⓒ more movement ⓓ *a tempo*

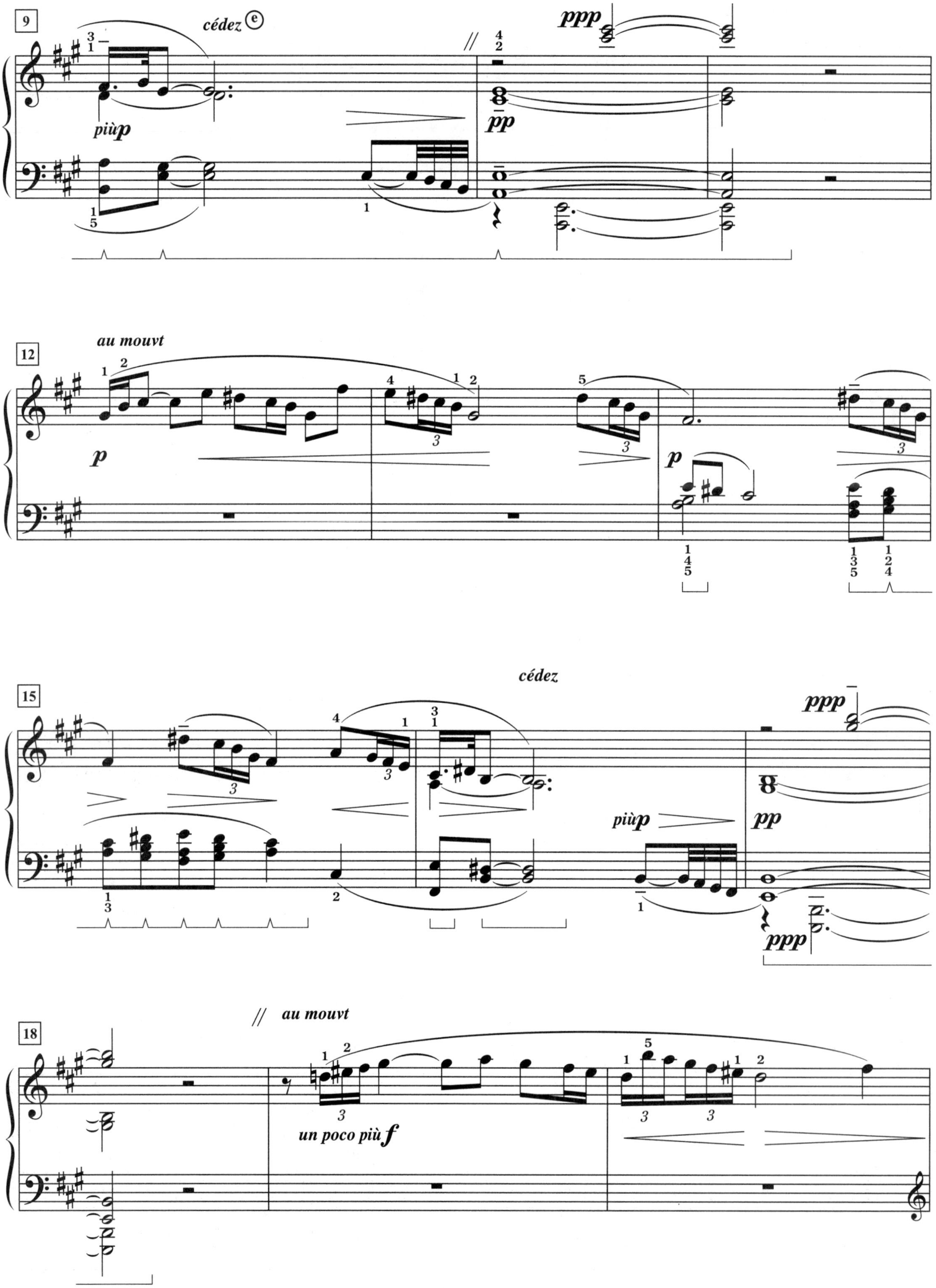
9
cédez ⓔ
più p
ppp
pp
12
au mouvt
p
15
cédez
più p
ppp
18
au mouvt
un poco più f

ⓔ slowing

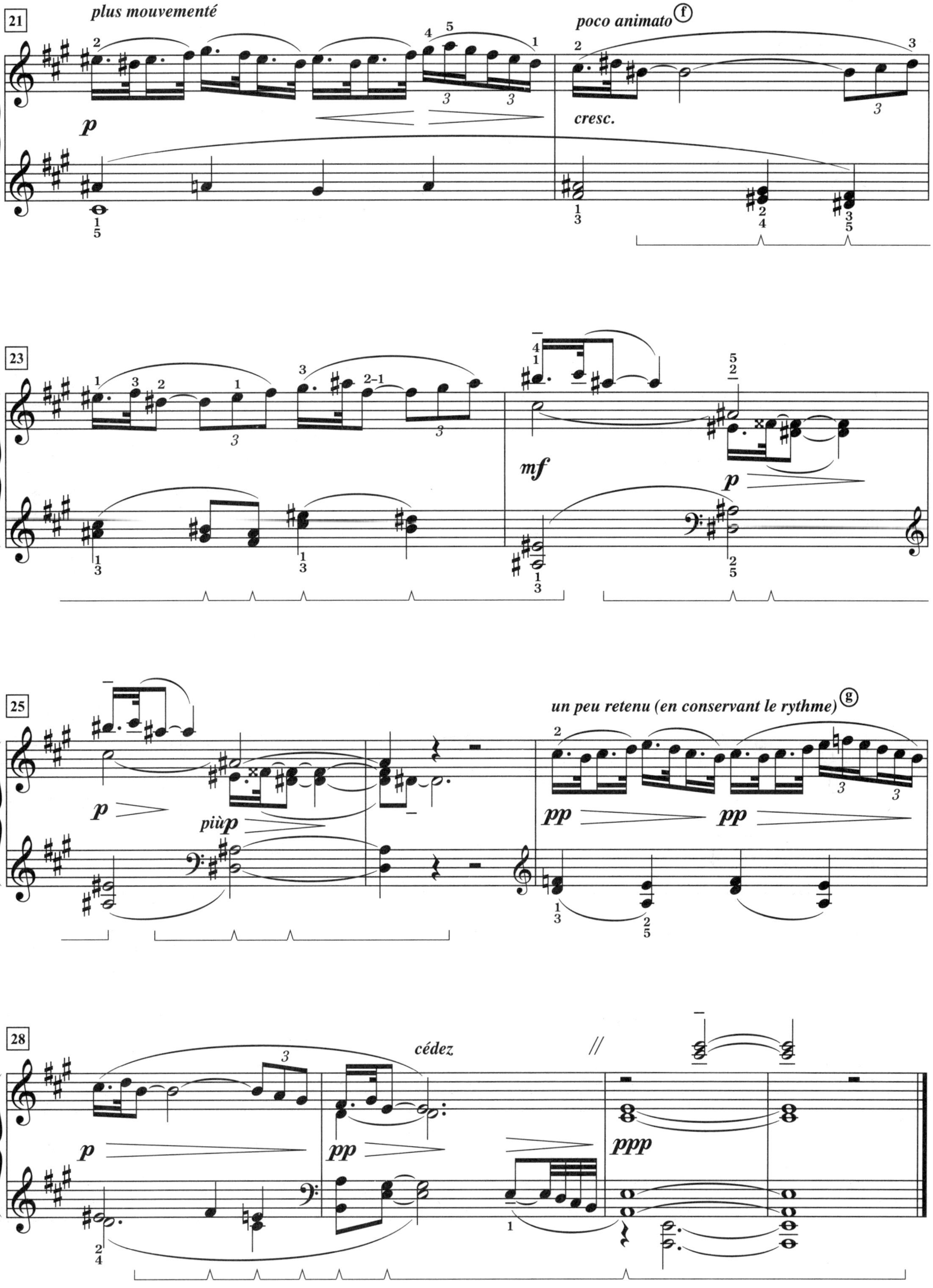

(f) a little livelier (g) hold back a little (maintaining the rhythm)

Album Leaf

Claude Debussy

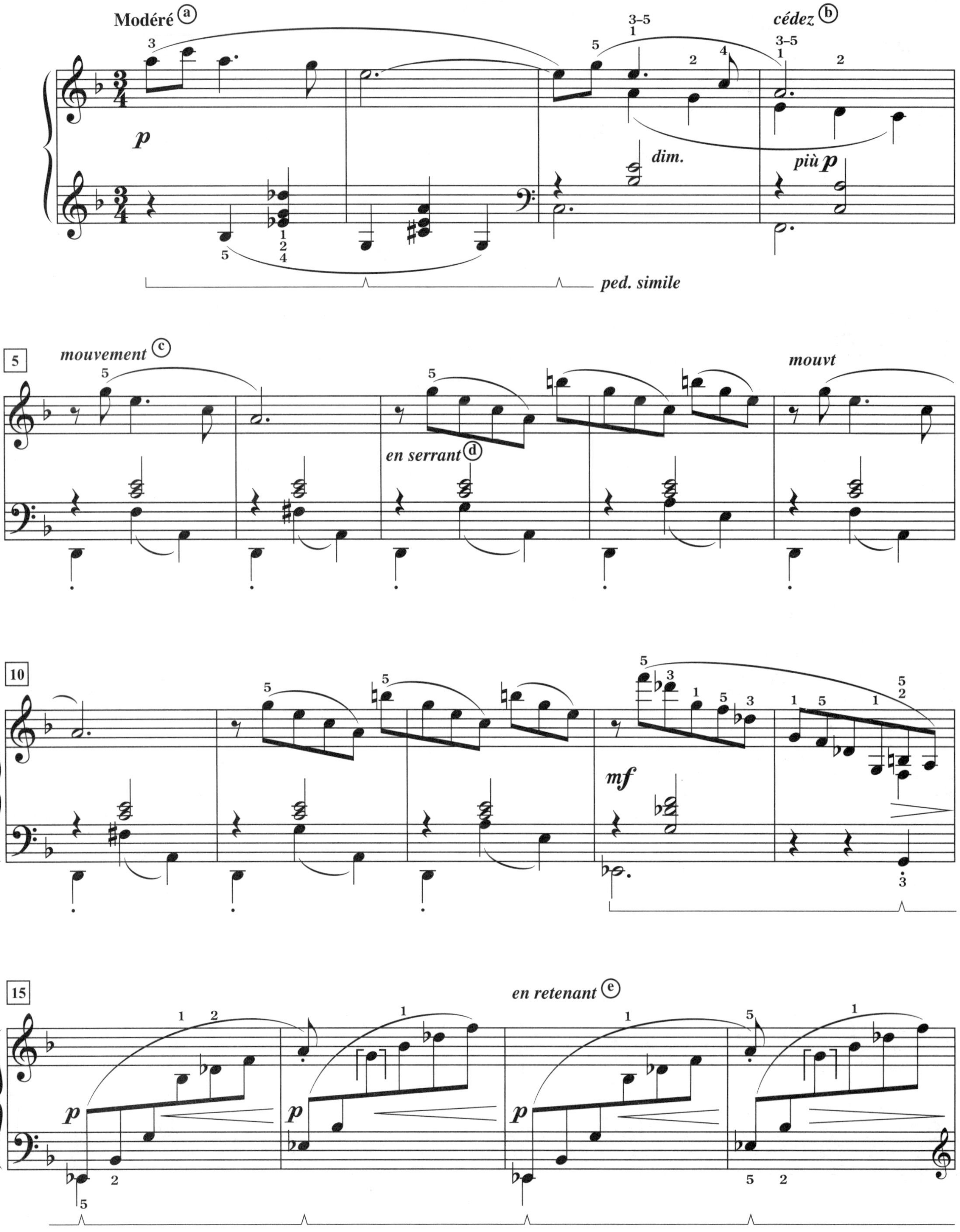

ⓐ moderately ⓑ hold back ⓒ *a tempo* ⓓ press forward ⓔ slowing down

ⓕ a little more lively

Brâul ⓐ

(No. 2 from Roumanian Folk Dances, Sz. 56)

Béla Bartók

ⓐ Waistband Dance

ⓑ Pedaling is Bartók's.

Buciumeana (a)

(No. 4 from Roumanian Folk Dances, Sz. 56)

Béla Bartók

(a) Dance from Butschum

(b) Pedaling is Bartók's.

The Farewell

Op. 21, No. 3

Sergei Bortkiewicz

Andantino dolente

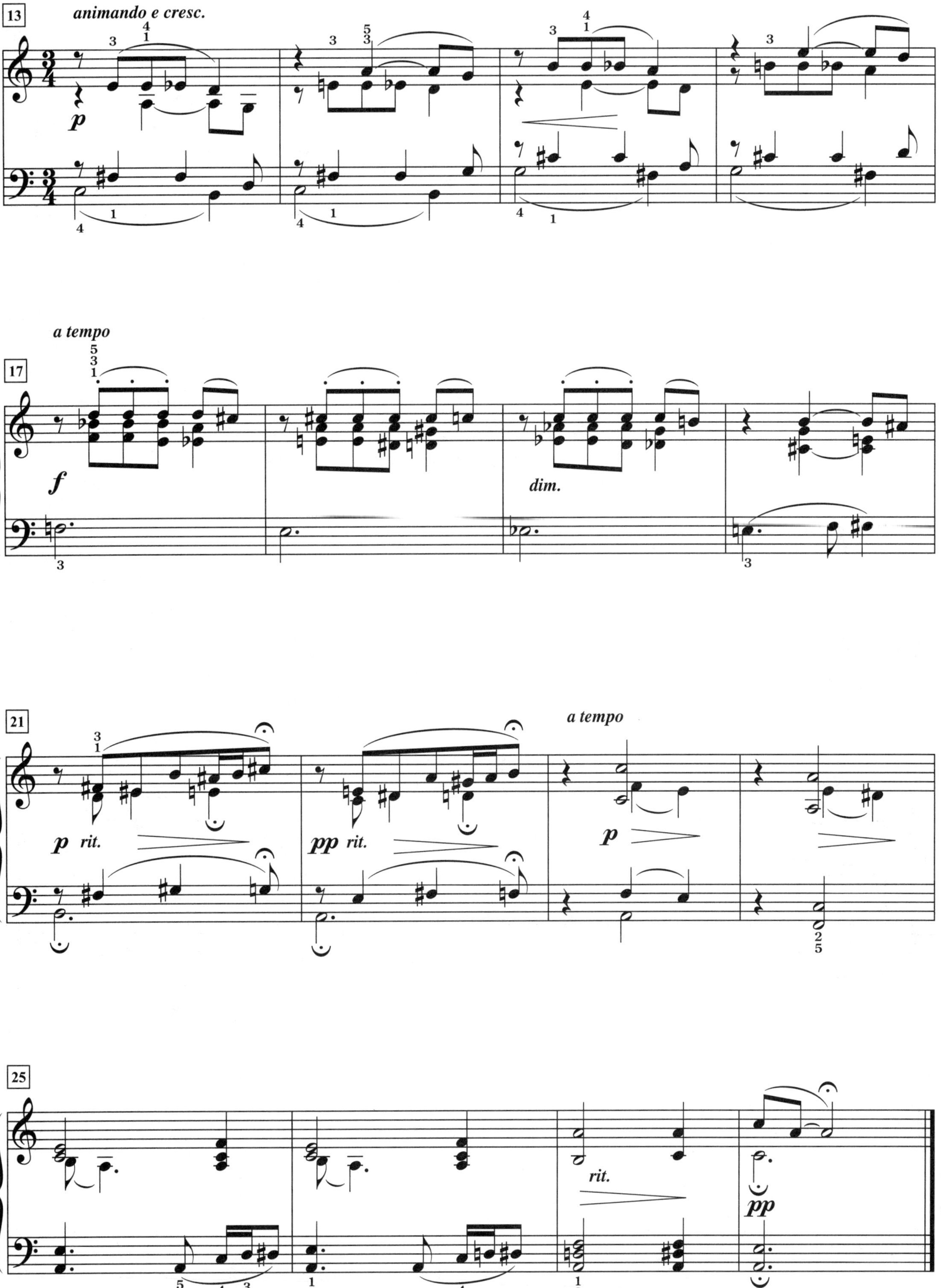
13
animando e cresc.
17
a tempo
dim.
21
rit.
rit.
a tempo
25
rit.

Venice

Song of the Gondolier, Op. 21, No. 7

Sergei Bortkiewicz

Ⓐ Use half pedals ad libitum in the left-hand ostinato sections to achieve a slightly blurred effect.

30
cresc.
f
37
dim.
pp
una corda
43
49
54
p
tre corde

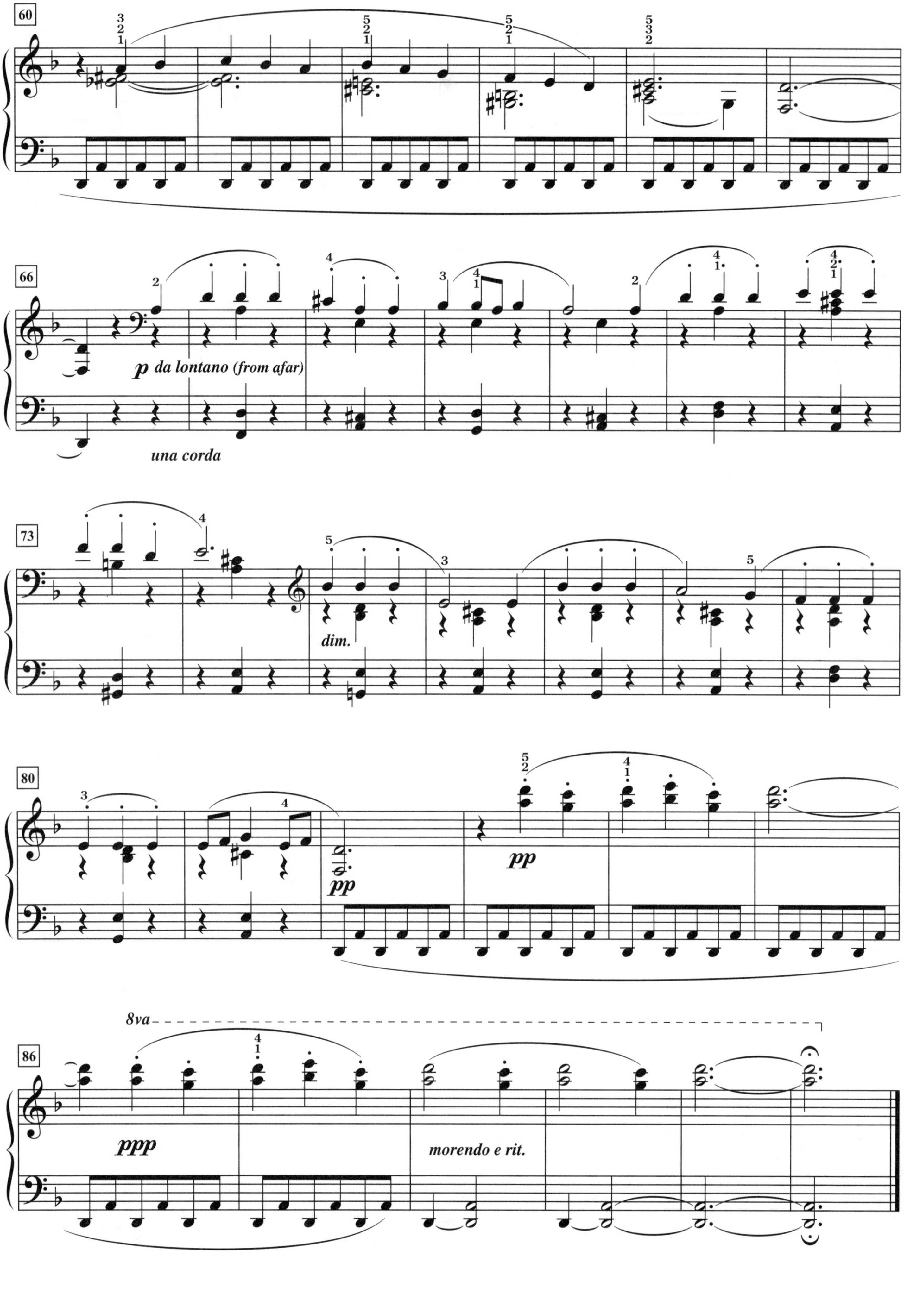
60
66
p da lontano (from afar)
una corda
73
dim.
80
pp
pp
8va
86
ppp
morendo e rit.

Pierrot's Serenade

Bohuslav Martinů

23
8va
dim.
mf
28
33
poco rit.
40
Tempo I
p
45
mf

50
55
Poco animato
8va
f
60
mf
dim.
p
65
poco a poco ritard.
p
70
dim.
pp

Columbine Remembers

Bohuslav Martinů

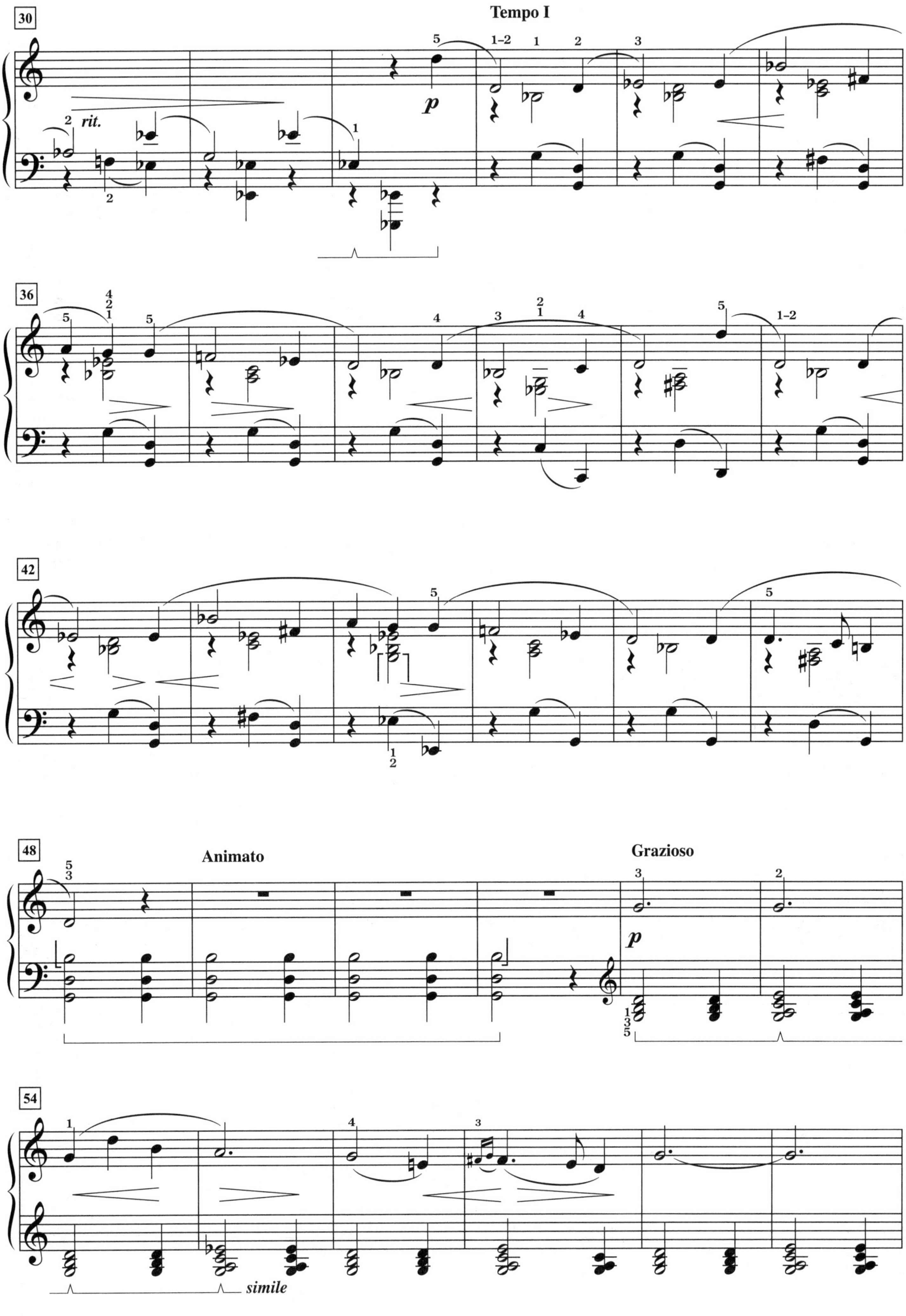
30
Tempo I
rit.
p
36
42
48
Animato
Grazioso
p
54
simile

60
66
73
p
mf
p
79
mf
p
mf
8va
85
f
ff

Tempo I
poch. rit.
sostenuto
sostenuto
Più animato
espress.

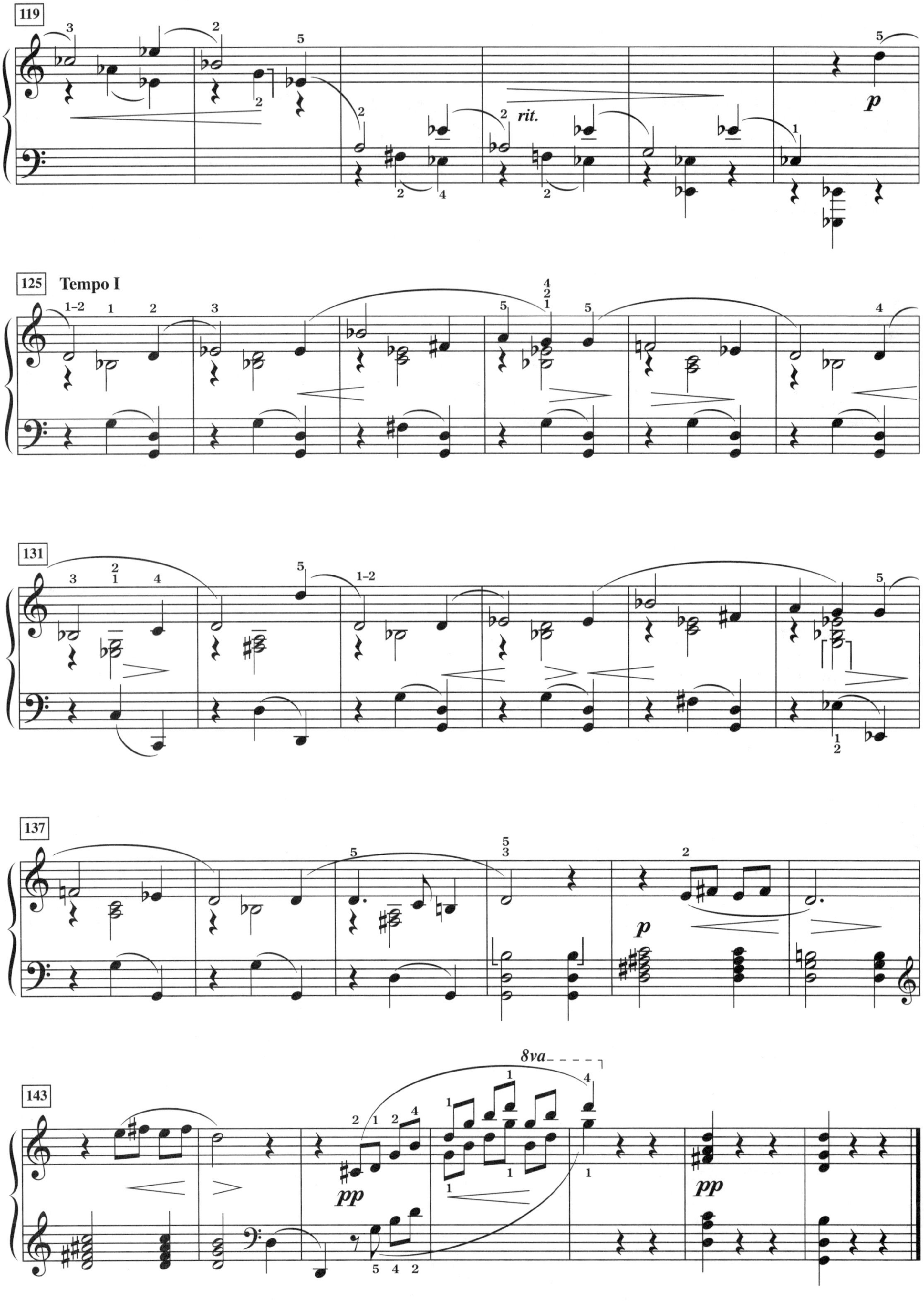
119
rit.
p
125
Tempo I
131
137
p
143
8va
pp
pp

Prelude (Fragment)[a]

(January 1925)

By George Gershwin

(a) This fragment of a prelude was used as part of the third movement of Gershwin's *Concerto in F*.

(b) The tied G's in measures 8 and 9 may be repeated.

Merry Andrew

By George Gershwin

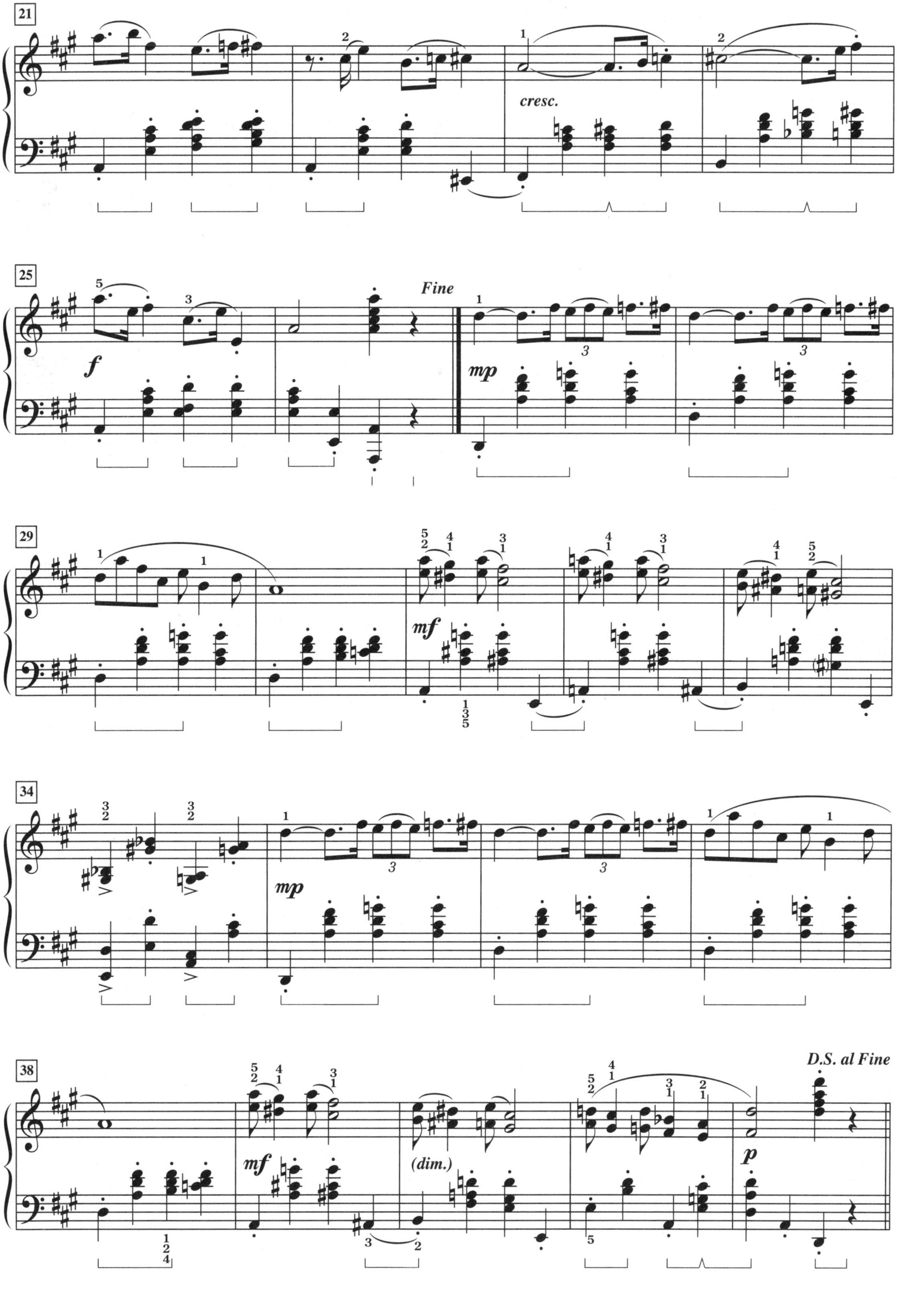
21
cresc.
25
f
Fine
mp
29
mf
34
mp
38
mf
(dim.)
D.S. al Fine
p

Promenade (Walking the Dog)

Music by George Gershwin

18
mf
21
24
27
mp
31

35
39
43
f
dim.
47
mf
50

53
p
f
56
mf
59
62
dim.
66
p

Composer Biographies

Johann Sebastian Bach (1685–1750, Germany) was a composer and organist. Born in Eisenach, Germany, he studied several musical disciplines as a boy, including violin, harpsichord, clavichord, organ and singing. He composed many keyboard works, including the 48 Preludes and Fugues from the *Well-Tempered Clavier* Books 1 and 2, 6 *French Suites,* 6 *English Suites* and 6 *Partitas* (all sets of dances), *Inventions* for two and three voices, and numerous other keyboard works. The *Notebook for Anna Magdalena Bach* from 1725 was probably a gift from the composer to his wife Anna Magdalena.

Domenico Scarlatti (1685–1757, Spain, born Italy), born in the same year as Handel and Bach, lived most of his life in Portugal and Spain. From 1720 to 1725 Scarlatti was court harpsichordist to the King of Portugal and teacher of his daughter Princess Maria Barbara, remaining her teacher even after she moved to Madrid in 1727. Her skill as a performer was likely the inspiration for his over 500 single-movement keyboard sonatas, which were innovative in the use of unusual keyboard techniques, such as crossed hands and rapid repeated notes.

Wolfgang Amadeus Mozart (1756–1791, Austria) composed in many musical mediums with equal brilliance, and was one of the greatest child prodigies ever. Mozart began to compose at the age of five by writing pieces for keyboard, and from then on composed quickly and easily. At the age of nine he composed his first choral piece, and composed his first opera at age 12.

Franz Joseph Haydn (1732–1809, Austria) was 24 years older than Mozart, yet outlived him by 18 years. Haydn produced an enormous output of music, including 47 keyboard sonatas and 104 symphonies. For nearly 50 years he was in the service of Prince Esterházy, a wealthy Hungarian nobleman. He was the supreme example of a royal court musician, having at his disposal a full orchestra of musicians to try out his musical ideas. He was called "Papa Haydn" by his friends in appreciation of his likable personality and good sense of humor.

Ludwig van Beethoven (1770–1827, Germany) was born in Bonn and grew up in a musical home. He began piano study at a young age and was a keyboard virtuoso by the time he had reached adulthood; at one point he was known as the greatest pianist of his time. The sense of humor in his music was more offbeat than the cheerful humor of Haydn. Throughout his music one finds sudden shifts in emotion and numerous surprises through changes of rhythm, key and dynamics.

Franz Schubert (1797–1828, Austria) was at the center of a circle of devoted friends who were leading writers, dramatists, singers, painters and poets in Vienna. Some of these friends held evening musicales, or so-called "Schubertiaden," at which only the works of Schubert were performed. Often Schubert himself would play the piano during these evenings, sometimes accompanying dancers, and improvise waltzes, ländler and écossaises. He is known for writing long, lyrical, and quite beautiful melodic lines.

Robert Schumann (1810–1856, Germany), born in Zwickau, began piano lessons at the age of six. His piano works primarily consist of sets of short pieces with descriptive titles—character pieces. Robert fell in love with, and eventually married Clara Wieck, a concert pianist and daughter of his piano teacher who did not approve of the courtship. Schumann wrote secret messages to Clara through motives in his compositions.

Frédéric Chopin (1810–1849, Poland) was born in the same year as Schumann and composed almost exclusively for the piano. He was one of the few truly great composers to achieve distinction solely by writing piano music. At the age of 20, he left his native Poland to live in Paris, where he made a career as a performer, teacher and composer. The popularity of many of his mazurkas, waltzes, nocturnes and polonaises brought Chopin great fame.

Edvard Grieg (1843–1907, Norway) stands at the forefront of those composers who wrote in a Nationalistic idiom. Many of his pieces are based on Norwegian folk music. The pieces included in this book are all from his sets of *Lyric Pieces*, some of the greatest character pieces in piano teaching literature. Grieg wrote that his objective in arranging the folk tunes of his native land was to raise them to the level of art music. His music displays a great deal of poetic fantasy.

Claude Debussy (1862–1918, France) was one of the most original and influential musical geniuses of all time. His compositions represent the epitome of Impressionism in music. As opposed to the bold statements and clarity of Germanic music, Impressionistic compositions tended to hint at ideas and featured an emphasis on color and atmosphere.

Béla Bartók (1881–1945, Hungary) was both a concert pianist and composer. He traveled throughout Rumania and Slovakia listening to and recording folks songs of the people of those regions. Bartók's music often uses Hungarian and other folk tunes as its basis. He wrote numerous educational piano works including *Mikrokosmos* and *For Children*, Books 1 and 2.

Sergei Bortkiewicz (1877–1952, Ukraine) studied both law and music, receiving his advanced training at the Imperial Conservatory in St. Petersburg. He composed in the style of Chopin, Liszt, Tchaikovsky and Rachmaninoff, and did not consider himself a modernist. The two pieces in this book are from his collection entitled *The Little Wanderer*, Op. 21, which is a series of pieces that reflect on the stages of an individual's travel.

Bohuslav Martinů (1890–1959, Czechoslovakia) is one of the most important 20th-century Czech composers, who made substantial contributions to the piano repertoire. The two pieces in this book are from a set of three books entitled *Puppets*, in which the music describes various aspects of a puppet's character. During World War II, Martinů resided in the United States.

George Gershwin (1898–1937, United States) was a popular American composer who was involved in the worlds of both pop music and concert music. Gershwin was a highly energetic person who loved parties where he could play the piano and sing his own songs for friends. *Promenade*, included in this book, was written for a film sequence titled "Walking the Dog." Gershwin's famous *Rhapsody in Blue*, composed in 1924, combined elements of jazz and the classical piano concerto, and is one of his most frequently performed works.